TREATMENT PLANNING IN CAREER COUNSELING

John J. Liptak

Brooks/Cole
Thomson Learning™

Australia • Canada • Mexico • Singapore • Spain
United Kingdom • United States

Counseling Editor: Julie Martinez
Editorial Assistant: Marin Plank
Marketing Manager: Caroline Concilla
Signing Representative: Ron Shelley
Project Editor: Matt Stevens
Print Buyer: April Reynolds

Permissions Editor: Robert M. Kauser
Production Service: Gustafson Graphics
Copy Editor: Linda Ireland
Cover Designer: Yvo Riezebos
Compositor: Gustafson Graphics
Printer: Webcom Limited

Printed in Canada
4 5 6 7 06 05

For permission to use material from this text, contact us by
  Web: http://www.thomsonrights.com
  Fax: 1-800-730-2215
  Phone: 1-800-730-2214

For more information, contact
Wadsworth/Thomson Learning
10 Davis Drive
Belmont, CA 94002-3098
USA
http://www.wadsworth.com

International Headquarters
Thomson Learning
International Division
290 Harbor Drive, 2nd Floor
Stamford, CT 06902-7477
USA

UK/Europe/Middle East/South Africa
Thomson Learning
Berkshire House
168-173 High Holborn
London WC1V 7AA
United Kingdom

Asia
Thomson Learning
60 Albert Street, #15-01
Albert Complex
Singapore 189969

Canada
Nelson Thomson Learning
1120 Birchmount Road
Toronto, Ontario M1K 5G4
Canada

Library of Congress Cataloging-in-Publication Data
Liptak, John J.
    Treatment planning in career counseling / by John Liptak.
        p. cm.
    Includes bibliographical references.
    ISBN 0-534-54985-3
        1. Vocational guidance.   2. Counseling.   I. Title.
HF5381.L53 2000
158.7—dc21   00-020257

 CONTENTS

 # PREFACE

There is a plethora of theory books available for career counselors and other helping professionals to use in their work with clients. Unfortunately, none of these texts show users how to implement these theories into practice. What is needed is a simple, practical book that integrates all the theories of career development into practice. The framework I have chosen for this integration of theories is the treatment planning process.

Treatment planning models for conducting psychotherapy are plentiful. No models are available, however, to assist career counseling professionals in the development of a plan for helping clients solve their career-related problems. This book, therefore, addresses the need of beginning and experienced career counselors by providing a process-oriented, "how-to" introductory text for providing career counseling services. A thorough discussion of each of the theories of career development is left for other texts. This book provides helping professionals with a review of the most influential career development theories and then illustrates how to use these theories in the development of treatment plans for career counseling.

To accomplish its purpose, the book groups the theories according to their emphasis in the career counseling process and uses the theories as a basis for conceptualizing the career-related problems of clients. In addition, readers are shown a treatment planning process that is effective in career counseling. The chapter contents include steps in conducting an intake interview, gathering personal and career information, the assessment process, and the process of developing goals, objectives, and interventions for each client.

A single client named Kathy is followed throughout the entire career counseling process. This case study helps to illustrate and hopefully "bring to life" the theories, as well as the treatment planning process in career counseling. It also seeks to highlight the interaction between theory and practice of career counseling. The last chapter, however, takes the reader through the entire treatment planning and career counseling process for another client in the hope that it will be beneficial to see the uninterrupted treatment planning process.

I am indebted to many people whose support I have had during the writing of this book. I am most grateful to my wife, Kathy, who not only encouraged and supported me but also worked hard to make it possible for me to have the free time to complete this project. For that, I am eternally grateful. I am grateful to the reviewers who offered helpful suggestions: Lorrie D. Anderson, Richland College; Camille De Bell, Texas Tech University; LeeAnn Eschbach, University of Scranton; Stephen S. Feit, Idaho State University; Margaret Pinder, Amber University; and Ann D. Puryear Scheer, Eastern Arizona College. A special thanks to the staff at Brooks/Cole with whom it has been a pleasure to work. A very special thanks to Eileen Murphy and Julie Martinez for their support and encouragement, insightful suggestions, and resources to complete this book. Lastly, I would like to thank my parents, John and Betty Liptak, and my sister Sue Ann and her family for their love and support throughout my educational endeavors.

ABOUT THE AUTHOR

John J. Liptak is Chair of the Behavioral Science Division at Wilmington College in New Castle, Delaware. He has authored four assessment instruments that have been published by JIST Publishing including the *Career Exploration Inventory, Leisure/Work Search Inventory, Barriers to Employment Success Inventory,* and the *Job Search Attitude Inventory.* John has also had six articles published in journals and has presented at numerous state, regional, and national conferences.

 PART ONE

THE NEED FOR TREATMENT PLANS

CHAPTER 1

INTRODUCTION

This book was written for career development and career counseling courses for undergraduate and graduate students in the helping professions. In addition, this book would be a valuable resource for students in field placement seminar courses. It helps students to integrate theory and practice by teaching a treatment planning model for career counselors. Because of the complexity of career development in today's society, career counseling has become much more complicated than the "test them and tell them" approaches of the past.

This book will help students learn to conceptualize their cases based on existing theories of career development, develop a comprehensive treatment plan for their clients, and choose interventions based on the needs of each individual client. By presenting an overview of the key concepts of each theory and describing how these theories fit into a treatment plan, students will be able to wisely select interventions that will help them to develop their own personal style of career counseling.

The format of this book is a survey of the major approaches to career counseling proposed as a model for developing effective treatment plans in career counseling. Therefore, instead of merely presenting the theoretical foundations and concepts of the models, the book presents the approaches in terms of how they can be used to assess the problems presented by your clients and to develop practical treatment plans. Through this format, the book not only will help you develop a comprehensive view of the major theories of career counseling but will also demonstrate how to implement interventions from each of the theories.

Treatment Planning in Career Counseling proposes that the best way for beginning students to learn the theories and techniques of career counseling is through a practical treatment planning approach. Because career counseling has become so complex, it is very difficult to translate theory into practice. No one theory by itself is sufficient in providing effective career counseling. The contributions of formal theories of career development to the practice of career counseling have been too numerous to measure. Current theories of career development, however, have several inadequacies. Borow (1982) categorized these deficiencies as scope limitations, methodological problems, and problems of practical application of the theories in counseling. Similarly, Crites (1981) contended that most career development theories focus strictly on career behavior. Although career counselors primarily focus on a client's career-related problems, there are often personal or interpersonal problems that are related to the client's career development. Another problem that has been identified in the literature recently has been the lack of theory directed toward women and people from various minority groups. This can be seen in the increasing number of articles dealing with the career development of people from other cultures (Leong, 1991; Parker, 1991), the career development of African Americans (Cheatham, 1990; Hawks & Muha, 1991), and the career development of women in the workforce (Gainor & Forrest, 1991; Read, Elliot, Escobar, & Slaney, 1988).

Given these problems with theories, it is very difficult for most career counselors to translate theory into practice. Many authors (e.g., Jepsen, 1984; Osipow, 1983) have attempted to classify the many existing theories of career development. The primary purpose of this book is to help you classify the current theories of career development and to integrate them into a systematic career counseling model that is uniquely your own. Your model should be congruent with your thoughts about career development and your beliefs about the career development process.

Gysbers and Associates (1984) contend that career counselors' informal theories are derived from their personal experiences and their counseling experiences. Furthermore, they suggest that the practice of career counseling should be geared to the individual needs of the clients. Therefore, the best delivery system of career counseling is through an integrated, eclectic approach.

WHO THIS BOOK IS FOR

Career counselors help people to make and implement effective career decisions. Most other counselors, however, whether or not they consider themselves employment counselors, also encounter situations in which they are required to help their clients deal with career issues. The rehabilitation counselor who helps people with physical and psychological disabilities, the mental health counselor who works with a client suffering from depression because she hates her job, and the substance abuse counselor who helps his client find permanent, full-time employment that would interfere with a return to drinking—all these counselors are faced with employment issues every day. Dealing appropriately with employment issues can make the difference between effective and ineffective counseling services.

The primary purpose of this book is to help counselors develop the basic skills and knowledge needed to effectively deal with their clients' employment problems. Some counselors will choose to specialize in employment counseling, thus devoting much of their career to helping people deal with the stress of unemployment and helping people find fulfilling employment. Other counselors, though, will train as generalists and work with many different types of clients with many types of problems. These counselors will address employment problems as they arise with their clients. Counselors trained as generalists will find valuable information in this book for adapting their skills to the needs of their clients with employment problems.

Many helping professionals, in addition to career counselors, are being called upon to help people with their "career problems." Examples of these helping professionals include licensed counselors, social workers, psychologists, school guidance counselors, mental health counselors, addictions counselors, employment counselors, and psychiatrists. These professionals often find themselves doing career counseling. For example, a school guidance counselor may assist students in identifying interests, choosing a college major, and identifying colleges to attend. A psychologist may administer a career assessment battery to a client who is indecisive about which career path to follow. A mental health counselor may need to do career counseling with a client who is depressed because he or she is underutilized in his or her current job. A psychologist is forced to deal with clients who may be unhappy partially because they do not like their jobs or are not suited for their jobs.

Another group of helping professionals who are called upon to provide assistance with career counseling and guidance is teachers, managers, job search specialists, and employment specialists. For example, teachers are frequently asked questions from students about whether the student should go to college or vocational school. Human resource managers are often asked about the best career path within a corporation. These examples illustrate the numerous times that helping professionals other than career counselors are asked for help in managing career development. Thus, this book can be effective as a "how-to" guide for people who may have some training in counseling, but who need to learn some career counseling skills so that they can apply the skills in their own work setting. Although these people have their own specialities, each of them is often called upon to provide assistance with career counseling.

BASIS OF THIS BOOK

This book enables the career counselor to develop a systematic approach to the career counseling process. By learning the career counseling process, you will have the skills needed to respond with career counseling interventions based on the needs of your clients. Every part of the career counseling process described in this book will not be appropriate for you.

The intention is to give you alternatives in developing treatment plans for your clients.

Because of the complexity of career counseling and the limitations of current theories of career development, what is needed for effective practice is a systematic method of using these theories as a diagnostic system in developing treatment plans. Following are five critical tasks that individuals must complete in order to make and implement career decisions. These critical tasks integrate the major career counseling models and serve to structure the career counseling interview, to categorize the major theories of career development, and to structure the remaining sections of this book

1. Career choice is a developmental process that encompasses one's work and one's leisure experiences over a period of time. The theories that have influenced this belief are Ginzberg's developmental theory, Blau and Duncan's status attainment theory, and Super's life-span, life-space theory.

2. People continually acquire and process accurate, as well as inaccurate, career information about themselves and the world. This information is gained through a variety of life experiences and often forces people to operate under inaccurate suppositions about themselves and the world-of-work. The theories that have influenced this belief are Hackett and Betz's self-efficacy approach to career development, Krumboltz's social learning theory, and Peterson, Sampson, and Reardon's cognitive information-processing model of career choice.

3. Career choice ultimately involves a matching of the characteristics of the individual with those of the work environment. The theories that have influenced this belief are Holland's theory of vocational choice, Roe's early childhood theory, and Parson's trait-factor approach.

4. Most people do not possess a systematic, logical method for making career-related decisions. They often need to address the psychological traits related to their decision-making style and the barriers related to career decision making. The theories that have influenced this belief are Vroom's expectancy model, Janis and Mann's conflict model, and Tiedeman's theory of career decision making.

5. All people experience, or hope to experience, intrapersonal and interpersonal satisfaction from the work they do. The better the match between a person and the occupation, the more the person will experience life satisfaction. The theories that have influenced this belief are Hershenson's model of work adjustment, Liptak's leisure theory of career development, and Lofquist and Dawis's theory of work adjustment.

As I have proposed, career development, choice, and adjustment to an occupation is a very complex process. None of the current theories of career development are comprehensive in nature. Therefore, the practicing career counselor must learn to integrate the best techniques from the various theories for appropriate interventions. This can be a difficult task not only for the beginning career counselor but also for the experienced career counselor. The five premises listed previously provide the structure needed for an eclectic approach to the career counseling interview. This approach allows the career counselor to look at the client in a holistic manner.

OVERVIEW OF THE BOOK

This book deals with treatment planning as it relates to the practice of career counseling. Each chapter contains a dialogue between the career counselor and a client. This internal dialogue will help to illustrate the use of the theories and techniques that are discussed. A case study of one client, Kathy, is used throughout the book to help to illustrate the entire career counseling process. The text provides you with the theory and techniques needed to work effectively with clients.

Part One describes the need for treatment planning from a career counseling perspective. Chapter 1 introduces the reader to the profession of career counseling. Chapter 2 introduces students to the complex nature of career counseling. Because the role of the career counselor has been expanded, the chapter includes information about changes in society and the world-of-work. In addition, you are introduced to Kathy, a client who is used throughout the book to demonstrate the development of a treatment plan in career counseling. Chapter 3 offers an overview of the need for and utility of treatment planning in career counseling. This part of the book helps readers to start thinking about how complex career counseling really is and provides a case for a treatment planning approach to help clients in career counseling.

Part Two describes the process for completing an intake assessment. Chapters 4 illustrates the process for gathering information. It concentrates on the process for gathering both personal and career information. Chapter 5 examines the relationship between the client and the career counselor. This chapter highlights how you can structure an interview for career counseling and some of the basic helping skills that will get the career counseling process started. It focuses on the basic skills that a counselor needs to be an effective career counselor. Chapter 6 examines helping the client assess self and the world-of-work.

Part Three describes treatment planning from the viewpoint of a variety of different theories. In order to develop a treatment plan, career counselors must first conceptualize each case. This is done by viewing the clients' career-related problems from the five different categories of career development theories. Therefore, Chapters 7 through 11 review a variety of ways of conceptualizing your clients' career problems: Chapter 7 examines a developmental point of view; Chapter 8 covers a cognitive point of view; Chapter 9 uses a matching point of view; Chapter 10 illustrates a decision-making point of view; and Chapter 11 examines an implementation and adjustment point of view. This book proposes that each theory of career development can be effective in the development of treatment plans. Therefore, each theory is reviewed with regard to its possible contribution to the treatment planning process. Evaluations of the individual theories are not provided.

Part Four illustrates the use of the treatment planning model and provides information about evaluation and termination. Chapter 12 demonstrates the use of the treatment planning model with a complete case study of a client based on an eclectic career counseling approach.

CHAPTER 2

THE COMPLEXITY OF CAREER COUNSELING

A new client named Kathy comes into your office. When you ask how you can help her, she replies, "I'm kind of depressed because I don't like my job. I've been a teacher for the past four years and I'm thinking of changing jobs, but I don't know what I want to do."

On the surface, Kathy's problem seems simple enough—help her find a job, and all will be well. The truth of the matter, however, is that there is a variety of problems with which this client needs help. The career counselor not only needs to help the client gather occupational information and make career decisions but also needs to assist the client in coping with her feelings of depression, managing her stress more effectively, and identifying effective ways of dealing with her health-related issues. Because of the many changes in society in general, and more specifically in the workplace, career counselors must rely on treatment plans to assist their clients.

CHANGES IN THE WORKPLACE

The matching model developed by Parsons at the turn of the twentieth century is still being used by some career counselors and job placement specialists. The matching model is a relatively simplistic approach to career counseling in which the career counselor administers a variety of assessment instruments, identifies traits of the client, and then matches those traits to similar factors in a variety of jobs. This model, however, does not seem sufficient for the kind of society in which we live. Hansen (1997) argues for the use of more broadly based approaches. She says that old matching approaches to career planning "were designed for a different period in time and society and have neglected or excluded (perhaps unconsciously) some of the critical personal issues influencing career development today" (p. 7).

The workplace of today has changed considerably and will continue to do so. Hansen (1997) suggests that the American workplace revolution has just begun. There is a plethora of information related to the consequences of the new workplace (c.f., Bridges, 1994; Charland, 1993). In order to understand this complexity, you need to understand the changes that have taken place in our society and in the world-of-work.

Loss of Work Role

During the 1990s, downsizing was a common practice among many companies in the private sector and agencies in the public sector. The rate of job loss was higher during the 1990s recovery than it was during the recession of the early 1980s. Gysbers, Heppner, and Johnston (1998) say that "job loss has economic meanings as well as social and psychological meanings" (p. 19).

Unemployment is one of the most stressful events in a person's life. Research indicates that the stress of unemployment can be linked to a variety of psychological disorders including depression (Feather & Davenport, 1981), suicide (Platt, 1984), alcoholism (Brenner, 1973), and child abuse (Weeks & Drencacz, 1983). Factors such as these then interfere with the job search process, which in turn can cause additional stress for the individual (Jones, 1979; O'Brien & Kabanoff, 1979). Many other studies have documented the ways in which unemployment has negatively influenced people's lives (Brenner & Bartell, 1983; Sinfield, 1981; Warr, Jackson, & Banks, 1982).

Winegardner, Simonetti, and Nykodym (1984) have described unemployment as "The Living Death"; they say that "unemployment can have a devastating impact on the human psyche, just as the major crises of divorce, the death of a loved one, and facing death itself strongly affect each individual" (p. 149). Their research suggests that the unemployed go through five stages that parallel those confronting individuals facing death or other serious emotional traumas (pp. 150–153). The stages are as follows.

Stage One: Denial and Isolation. In this stage, individuals deny that they have been terminated from or have lost their jobs. They may be confused about their job loss. They may be denying the fact that they are or soon will be out of a job. They may be saying to themselves such things as, "How can they do this to me? I've been a good employee." They are probably shocked by the realization that they are dispensable. They may have felt that the company could not get along without them. They are probably feeling inadequate and questioning their self-worth, and they may even be feeling guilty.

Stage Two: Anger. In this stage, the reality of the termination has registered, and individuals begin to feel anger toward the organization, management, and/or immediate supervisors. The union, the system, or foreign competition may later become the target of their discontent. Then, after they have expressed anger at all possible outside sources, their anger is turned inward. Self-analysis begins to become self-criticism. They may be saying to themselves such things as, "If only I had worked harder . . ." or "If I had studied a different subject in school, this would not have happened."

Stage Three: Bargaining. In this stage, individuals begin to calculate, compute, reflect, and compromise. They attempt to influence management—to bargain with the company or an immediate supervisor in an attempt to reverse the decision. As their attempts to compromise fail, they give up. They ask such questions as, "What can I do now?" They also try to identify their options. Their focus is on the future and on the possibilities that are available. They feel that when they get through this ordeal, they will be better people because of it.

Stage Four: Depression. In this stage, individuals focus more and more on their situation. They become more silent and withdrawn, thus contributing to feelings of depression. Because they have focused so much on being unemployed, they may feel a sense of meaninglessness. They are probably frustrated and doubting their abilities. They feel lethargic and simply want to be left alone. They are probably saying to themselves such things as, "There are no jobs available for me" or "Nobody cares what happens to me."

Stage Five: Acceptance. In this stage, individuals focus on the realities of the situation; analyze their skills, abilities, and resources; and face the future. They realize that their job is gone; they accept the fact that they no longer have a job and that it is time to get on with the task of searching for a new job. They experience more energy as they begin their job search. They have probably analyzed their skills and abilities and are generating a new "game plan." They have adjusted to being unemployed and are excited about getting on with their lives.

Increase in Technology

Technology is driving many of the new opportunities in the world-of-work. Personal computers and the Information Age have made it possible for everyone to have inexpensive access to tons of information, along with the ability to create such information and utilize it from almost anywhere. This increase in technology has made several very evident changes in the workplace.

First, no longer do all workers have to go to the company office to work. More work is being outsourced to employees who work from their homes. With the advent of computer and satellite technology, the need for workers to be technologically literate has increased. Workers are now using computer networks and team networks to do a great majority of their work. Eventually workers will rely on television and computers to meet all of their customer service needs. Hines (1994) believes that by the year 2010, we will be in the Infotech Society in which workers will do their work by computing combined with telecommunications and networking.

Second, technology has produced a variety of new jobs and entire industries including personal computer manufacturing, software development, video game development, biotechnology, and wireless telecommunications. In addition, technology has forever changed industries such as health care and financial services.

Third, changes are occurring in the way people work. Rifkin (1995) believes that computers will continue replacing jobs to the point that large numbers of people will not have work as we now know it. He suggests that not only will many jobs cease to exist, but we can also expect shorter work-weeks, a new social contract, an emphasis on the social economy, more volunteering, and more service to the nonprofit community.

Finally, robots will continue to replace workers in the next millennium. Robots, which traditionally have been used strictly for factory positions, will continue to replace workers in a variety of industries. Although robotic technology has existed for years, we are rapidly understanding the true impact of robots in the workplace.

It has become apparent that for workers to be successful in our present society, they must be computer literate and knowledgeable about the technologies that impact their jobs.

Changing Organizations

In addition to mass downsizing, other major changes have taken place in the workplace. Wages over the last decade have steadily declined for the average worker. In addition, compensation plans have been affected so that employers are paying less toward employee pension plans and health insurance costs and employees are paying more for these benefits. To cut costs and improve efficiency, most major companies also have begun to use temporary workers. The types of temporary workers include contractual workers, piecemeal workers, consultants, freelance workers, part-time workers, and outsource workers. Charland (1993) states that labor market estimates in the United States say that at least a third of all job roles are in transition, a third of all vocational-technical schools have become obsolete, and a third of all workers eventually leave their jobs. Transitions in the workplace have become commonplace. Most companies even have career and outplacement services as a part of their human resource departments.

Globalization

Another change that has occurred is the decreased number of jobs available for today's workforce. Many workers today have been, or worry about being, laid off from their jobs. Several reasons for this concern among workers include the facts that many companies have streamlined their operations and released unnecessary labor, moved their operations to countries outside the United States due to the low cost of labor there, and replaced their workforce with computers, robots, and other production-efficient technology. Until the mid-1950s, the majority of people worked for one employer their whole life and never had to worry about being downsized.

Increase in Self-Employment

Many authors contend that in the future, workers will change jobs more frequently; workers will be required to move more often to get a job; and workers will be required to retrain as a way of moving into new employment opportunities. Fewer people are now working for large corporations. In fact, more and more people are starting small businesses and working from home in home-based businesses. The number of franchises being started has increased, and the number of small businesses has doubled. The number of female-owned businesses is increasing faster than the number of those owned by males. In addition, the number of self-employed African Americans and Hispanic Americans has increased tremendously over the last ten years. Some of the reasons for these trends include sharing jobs with another employee, compressed weekends, the use of flextime, reduced work hours, increase in the use of temporary workers, an increase in the use of volunteers, and participatory management.

Changing Demographics

The United States Department of Labor (1993) has indicated that the number of Hispanics and Asians in the labor force will continue to increase at a much faster rate than the number of white non-Hispanics. Similarly, the number of African Americans in the labor force will grow slightly faster than the rest of the workforce. In addition, the number of women entering the workforce will continue to be at a much faster rate than the entry rate for men. An increasingly diverse society and workplace will require career counselors to understand and be able to provide services to people with differences—whether those differences are in religion, ethnicity, race, gender, age, class, diversity, or sexual orientation.

Hansen (1997) believes that "interpersonal relationships always have been important both on and off the job, but in the future career professionals will have to pay even greater attention to helping individuals build mutual respect, trust, and self-esteem and value differences" (p. 9). Similarly, Brown and Minor (1992) believe that career assistance has focused primarily on white middle-class populations, but that career professionals now need new theories and techniques to effectively interact with diverse populations in the workplace.

Because there have been so many changes in the workplace, career counselors have had to alter their practices. These practices include the way career counselors now define a career, what comprises career counseling, and the need to develop treatment plans to direct the career counseling process.

CHANGES IN THE CAREER COUNSELING PROFESSION

Many changes are taking place in the practice of career counseling. These changes are directing the way career counselors approach their practice. One major change is that career counseling now often includes personal counseling. Our client, Kathy, not only needs assistance in making career decisions, but she also needs assistance in coping with the stress and depression she is feeling. In order to assist her with these issues, the career counselor must have expertise in personal counseling techniques as well as career counseling techniques.

The connection between career counseling and personal growth is well established (Imbimbo, 1994; Krumboltz, 1994). Krumboltz (1994) believes that there is a correlation between career and personal adjustment in that clients who make effective career decisions gain skill and confidence that may spill over as they confront other problem areas. He concludes that the two are intertwined and are often treated together. Similarly, Brown (1985) believes that career counseling may be a viable option for clients who have emotional problems related to stressful environments.

Personal counseling or psychotherapy has been described as an intensive process whereby a helping professional assists people to cope with their problems. Crites (1981) was one of the first theorists who believed that comprehensive career counseling incorporates the best from theories of counseling and psychotherapy and even goes beyond them. He based this belief on the following five propositions:

1. The need for career counseling is greater than the need for psychotherapy.
2. Career counseling can be therapeutic.
3. Career counseling should follow psychotherapy.
4. Career counseling is more effective than psychotherapy.
5. Career counseling is more difficult than psychotherapy.

Crites believed that career counseling not only facilitates career development, career choice, and career adjustment, but it also enhances the personal adjustment of the client. He said that "career counseling often embraces personal counseling but it goes beyond this to explore and replicate the client's role in the main area of life—the world of work" (p. 11).

Yost and Corbishley (1987), in their book *Career Counseling: A Psychological Approach,* suggest that for some clients, personal counseling and career counseling are virtually synonymous. They contend that "the psychological constraints affecting career counseling express themselves in the form of dysfunctional emotions, behaviors, and cognitions" (p. 25).

Isaacson and Brown (1997) have said that a current trend is that career counseling will be increasingly recognized as a counseling specialization that requires counselors to have expertise in both career counseling and personal counseling. This claim can be verified by the many articles (e.g., Brown, 1985; Spokane, 1991) that have been written emphasizing the interrelationship between mental health and career concerns. Brown and Brooks (1991) contend that career counselors need to be highly skilled in both personal and career counseling to assist clients who come for career counseling and who need to work on psychological problems that inhibit them from making effective career choices.

Thus, framed in this light, psychotherapy should be an integral part of career counseling. Rarely will a client come to you for career counseling who does not have a variety of other concerns that go hand in hand with her occupational problems. Therefore, in today's society, career counselors must do more than "test them and tell them." Career counselors must be prepared to deal effectively with emotional problems that arise during the career counseling process.

CHANGES IN THE DEFINITION OF CAREER

One reason why career counseling is so complex is the lack of agreement about what constitutes a career. Therefore, before you can do career counseling, you must determine what you believe a career to be. There are many different definitions of a career. At one time, many career counselors viewed and defined a career as the job a person had. Similarly, many career counselors viewed career planning as fitting a person into the best available job. These definitions greatly limit clients and prevent them from exploring all the possibilities available to them by excluding all of life's roles. Still today, some authors, in describing a career, focus on the work that their clients have done. For example, Sears (1982) has described a career as the totality of work one does in a lifetime. Similarly, Isaacson and Brown (1997) have described a career as "a series of paid or unpaid occupations or jobs that one holds throughout his or her life" (p. 11). In today's society, however, these types of definitions seem to be too limiting in their view of career and career development as only the work one does. As can be seen in the example of Kathy at the beginning of the chapter, career-related problems can affect your client's relationships, home life, and leisure opportunities.

Many other authors, in recent years, have taken a more comprehensive view of what constitutes a career. Career has been seen as developmental in nature, and as encompassing much more than just one's vocation or occupation. Super (1951) first defined career as a "continuous, lifelong process of developing and implementing a self-concept, testing that self-concept against reality, with satisfaction to self and benefit to society" (p. 88). Later, he amended his definition to say that a career is the course of events that constitutes a life—the sequence of occupations and other life roles that combine to express a person's commitment to work in his or her total pattern of self-development (Super, 1976). Herr and Cramer (1984) have said that careers are unique to each person and include occupations and other life roles such as family, community, and leisure. McDaniels (1984) has described one's career as the totality of one's work and leisure over the life span. Similarly, Liptak (1992b) has taken the position that a career is each person's attempt to implement a particular lifestyle made up of work, leisure, and learning.

Most people can understand how work affects a client's career development. At this point, however, you are probably wondering how learning and leisure can affect your client's career development. Courses and classes taken can provide clients with new information and skills. A popular definition of leisure, proposed by Sears (1982), is that leisure consists of self-determined activities and experiences that are available due to having discretionary income, time, and social behavior. The activities may be physical, intellectual, volunteer, or creative, or some combination of these four. Thus, leisure activities can be very valuable in helping clients discover new skills and talents that may lead to additional career options.

The National Career Development Association (NCDA), formerly the National Vocational Guidance Association (NVGA), in defining career counseling, highlights the complexity of the process:

> Vocational/career counseling consists of those activities performed or coordinated by individuals who have credentials to work with other individuals or groups of individuals about occupations, life/career, career decision making, career planning, career pathing, or other career development related questions or conflicts. (National Vocational Guidance Association, 1982, p. 2)

The definitions related to careers and career development are extremely important as we now begin to shift our focus to theories of career development. The increase in the number of theories over the past ten years has expanded the way in which career counselors are working with their clients. In addition, I believe this increase in theorizing has extended the meaning of career development and has changed the focus of the career counselor.

We have learned throughout this chapter that there have been many changes in the workplace that impact career counseling. We also have learned that career development should be viewed from a holistic standpoint comprised of many factors. Sears (1982) viewed career development as the total constellation of psychological, sociological, educational, physical, economic, and chance factors that combine to shape the career of any given individual over the life span. This definition illustrates the number and type of factors that contribute to your client's career development.

 CHAPTER 3

TREATMENT PLANS IN CAREER COUNSELING

As can be seen in the case of Kathy, the client introduced in Chapter 2, career counseling is much more than simply giving tests to determine what type of occupation your clients are best suited for and providing feedback about the results of the tests. Beginning career counselors are often eager to simply learn several career counseling theories and some techniques from each theory so that they have a "quick-fix" solution to the clients' problems. This "quick-fix" attitude could be attributed to society's perception of career counseling as a "test them and tell them" method of counseling. Because career counseling has become more complex, the need for treatment planning becomes more evident.

THE NEED FOR TREATMENT PLANNING

Career counseling that has taken place in the past has often reflected the narrow "test them and tell them" approach. Since 1909 when Frank Parsons wrote *Choosing a Vocation,* the trait-factor approach has dominated the career counseling profession. This trait-factor approach utilizes the matching of the traits of the person with the important factors about the job. To accomplish this, the counselor often gives a variety of tests and makes suggestions about the best occupations for the client to consider in making career decisions. From its inception to about the 1960s, this approach was fairly effective. Today, however, a much more comprehensive approach is needed to help clients with career-related problems.

Crites (1981) refers to career counseling as an interpersonal process focused upon assisting an individual to make an appropriate career decision and adds that "ideally, it involves active participation in the decisional process, not simply passive-receptive input of information" (p. 11). Brown (1985) defines career counseling as "the process of helping an individual select, prepare for, enter, and function effectively in an occupation" (p. 197).

Thus, in your work as a career counselor, you will be called upon to assist clients not only with choosing an occupation to enter but also with career and life planning, decision making, and personal adjustment.

Career counselors can view their clients in a wide variety of ways. When working with their clients, career counselors must often use a variety of different perspectives. A comprehensive treatment plan should be developed on all clients based on their diagnosis.

According to the *Diagnostic and Statistical Manual of Mental Disorders* (DSM-IV), the intake interview, assessment, and development of a treatment plan are the first steps in effective counseling (American Psychiatric Association, 1994). The same is true for career counseling. Seligman (1993) has said:

> [T]reatment planning in counseling is the process of plotting out the counseling process so that both counselor and client have a road map that delineates how they will proceed from their point of origin (the client's presenting concerns and underlying difficulties) to their destination, alleviation of troubling and dysfunctional symptoms and patterns, and establishment of improved coping mechanisms and self-esteem. (p. 288)

Seligman (1996) has also said that treatment planning plays a variety of important roles in the counseling process by:

1. ensuring that counseling with a high likelihood of success is being provided,
2. allowing counselors to demonstrate accountability and effectiveness,
3. providing goals and procedures that can help counselors and clients track their progress, and
4. providing a sense of structure and direction to the counseling process.

Detailed written treatment plans can benefit not only the client, but also the career counselor. The client is served by having a written plan that details specific issues that will be the focus of the career counseling sessions. In this way, the career counselor does not lose sight of the most important issues that need to be addressed for client change. Treatment plans change and must be updated to reflect changes in the client's problem, goals, objectives, or interventions.

The career counselor is served by treatment plans because they force the counselor to think critically about the career counseling interventions that are best suited for clients to attain their goals. Because a formalized plan is developed to guide the career counseling process, career counselors are forced to "stay on track" and not stray from the client's stated goals and objectives. The career counselor must now pay more attention to technique and achieving results, and not simply "follow the client." A written, individualized career counseling treatment plan that has been reviewed and signed by the client can help career counselors stay focused and thus help to eliminate the threat of possible client litigation.

DEVELOPING A TREATMENT PLAN

A well-written treatment plan will clearly stipulate the client's presenting problems and the intervention strategies that will facilitate the career counseling process. For the plan to do so, however, the process of developing a plan must be consistent with all clients. Jongsma and Peterson (1995) insist that "the process of developing a treatment plan involves a logical series of steps that build on each other much like constructing a house" (p. 3). The foundation of career counseling treatment plans is the data gathered regarding how the problem presents itself in the client's life. During this process, the career counselor actively listens as the client tells his or her story. The counselor then tries to understand the issues in terms of the client's presenting problems.

This chapter presents the six phases for developing an effective treatment plan based on the assessment data presented by the client. Chapter 12 demonstrates the use of these six phases by a career counselor with an actual client.

Phase I: Intake Assessment

In career counseling sessions, clients are seen for intake interviews before treatment begins. Seligman (1996) has described the purposes of an intake interview as follows: to determine the suitability of the person for the counselor's services; to assess and respond to the urgency of the person's situation; to familiarize the person with the agency and the counseling process; to engender positive client attitudes toward counseling; and to gather sufficient client information. The focus of an intake interview is to gather enough information about the client to begin to formulate an effective treatment plan.

Phase II: Case Conceptualization

In this phase, the career counselor must conceptualize the most significant problems on which to start focusing the treatment plan. Each individual client will present his or her story in a unique manner with regard to how the problems present themselves. The career counselor will use the various theories of career counseling to identify specific symptom patterns that will become the focus of treatment.

The case conceptualization is the result of your intake interview and your assessments. It is equivalent to a diagnosis in psychotherapy, which is, admittedly, very subjective in nature. At this point, the career counselor will have attempted to collect as much detailed, specific information about the client as possible. The career counselor must now find a way of sifting through all this information. Mental health counselors are well aware of the importance of diagnosis and treatment planning in their work with clients. Seligman (1996) says that "diagnosis is an essential tool of the mental health counselor" (p. 55).

Mental health counselors can rely on the *Diagnostic and Statistical Manual of Mental Disorders* (DSM-IV; American Psychiatric Association, 1994). The *DSM-IV* lists diagnostic categories of disorders and describes the symptoms and behavior patterns found in each category. Each category also contains an identifying reference number. Mental health counselors can gather information about their clients' symptoms, behaviors, beliefs, and personal history and attempt to match this information with the criteria listed for various diagnostic categories. The counselors believe that if a client's symptoms and behaviors are similar to those of individuals with a particular diagnosis, they can assume that their client has that diagnosis. This process then aids in assessment and treatment planning.

Career counselors, however, do not have such a resource to guide their diagnoses. Stark (1998) says that good treatment planning requires assessment of the problem in light of the meaning that the counselor's orientation places on the problem and that "theoretical conceptualization is at the heart of good treatment planning" (p. 9). Therefore, career counselors must rely on the various theories of career development as a framework for diagnosing the client's presenting problem; this diagnosis, in turn, determines the goals, objectives, and interventions that will be established.

Case conceptualization is also the attempt by the career counselor to determine why the client has come in for career counseling. Many types of career problems have been identified in the literature (Crites, 1981; Isaacson & Brown, 1997). The client should be probed to determine how the client views his or her problems.

The model used in this text to develop a treatment plan breaks the important career-related issues for an individual into five categories. Because none of the current theories of career development are comprehensive in nature, the practicing career counselor must learn to pick and choose the best techniques from the various theories for appropriate interventions. These categories can be useful for the career counselor to use in identifying problems in the client's career development:

1. Career choice is a developmental process that encompasses one's work and one's leisure experiences over a period of time (developmental theories).

2. People continually acquire and process accurate, as well as inaccurate, career information about themselves and the world. This information is gained through a variety of life experiences and often forces people to operate under inaccurate suppositions about themselves and the world-of-work (cognitive theories).
3. Career choice ultimately involves a matching of the characteristics of the individual with those of the work environment (matching theories).
4. Most people do not possess a systematic, logical method for making career-related decisions. They often need to address the psychological traits related to their decision-making style and the barriers related to career decision making (decision-making theories).
5. All people experience, or hope to experience, intrapersonal and interpersonal satisfaction from the work they do. The better the match between a person and the occupation, the more the person will experience life satisfaction (implementation and adjustment theories).

The most critical part of treatment planning in career counseling is problem assessment and case conceptualization. In this process, the theories of career development reviewed in Chapters 7 through 11 are used as a means of identifying and diagnosing client career-related problems.

Phase III: Goal Development

The next step in the development of an effective treatment plan is the establishment of broad goals indicative of the client's problems. These goal statements should be expressed as global, long-term objectives that will guide the treatment procedures. For example, goal statements in career counseling treatment plans might include such global statements as, "Gather information about occupations of interest" or "Explore how the client makes career decisions."

Phase IV: Constructing Objectives

In this phase, the career counselor and client construct objectives. Objectives, unlike goals, must be specific and stated in behaviorally measurable terms. They are developed as a step toward attaining the client's broad treatment goals. Timetables should be identified for when the client is expected to achieve each established objective, and outcomes should be measurable to meet the demand for accountability. Each presenting problem may have multiple objectives, depending on the nature of the problem. The career counselor must exercise judgment about the appropriateness of each objective for the client.

Jongsma and Peterson (1995) argue that each objective should be developed in light of attaining a general treatment goal. They say that objectives can be thought of as a series of steps that will result in the achievement of the long-term goal when completed. They also recommend that each objective include a target date for attainment. As the client progresses in treatment, new objectives are added. The client's achievement of long-term goals is noted by the completion of the objectives for each goal.

Ginter (1995) identified a five-step process that can be used for establishing objectives:

1. Describe the problem as specifically as you can.
2. Transform the problem into an objective by stating it as something that needs to be done differently.
3. Make the objective measurable by stating it in terms of frequency, intensity, duration, or amount.
4. Establish the criteria for achieving the objective.
5. Identify a time frame for achieving each objective.

Phase V: Interventions

Interventions are the specific actions that will be taken by the career counselor to help the client achieve his or her goals and objectives. Specific interventions should be tied to the pattern symptom of the problem. Interventions from a broad range of therapeutic approaches should be used to help the client attain the objectives. Interventions are the heart of any treatment plan. The career counselor, at this point, will specify the techniques to be used to accomplish the objectives that have been identified. The techniques are thus linked to how each objective will be attained. At least one intervention for each objective should be listed. If an intervention does not help the client achieve the objective, new interventions should be identified based on the needs of the client and the career counselor's helping approach.

Phase VI: Evaluation and Termination

All interventions should be measured and evaluated in terms of their effectiveness in the treatment of the specific client problems. As the demand for accountability becomes greater, measurable objectives to evaluate success are being implemented. As the client's goals are attained, the last step in the process is the termination of the client–career counselor relationship.

The final phase of the career counseling process is evaluating any changes that have occurred, assessing the impact of the interventions that have been used, and eventually terminating the career counseling relationship. Gysbers, Heppner, and Johnston (1998) believe that "bringing meaningful closure to a counseling relationship is often a most difficult task for counselors" (p. 308). Part of the reason for this is that often both counselors and clients resist closure. You need to be aware of this uncomfortableness in yourself and in your clients. An open discussion of your feelings can be an effective way of helping your clients to overcome their feelings of resistance.

Brown and Brooks (1991) addressed this issue by describing three tasks that require the attention of the career counselor. The first task is to review the goals that have been developed in conjunction with the client and consolidate any new learning by the client. They suggest that the career counselor ask clients to review their goals and provide a summary in their own words of what has taken place during the career counseling process. At this point in the process, the career counselor may choose to revisit some of the original interventions or try some new interventions. The second task suggested by Brown and Brooks is to have clients explore any feelings they might have about terminating the career counseling relationship. The third task is preparation for the transfer of new learning from the career counseling process. Helping clients to follow through on what they have learned and implement their career plans is crucial for the success of career counseling.

Brown and Brooks (1991) caution career counselors not to terminate the client–career counselor relationship prematurely, before the clients have completed all of their objectives. They list several possible reasons for premature closures, including: (1) clients believe they have achieved their goals; (2) clients fear what they have discovered in the process of career counseling; (3) the career counseling process does not meet client expectations; and (4) the client was not very committed in the first place.

Similarly, Gysbers, Heppner, and Johnston (1998) list three primary reasons for closure, including that the counselor and client feel that the initial goals for career counseling have been met and there is no further need to meet; the client has decided not to take any actions at this time; and the pain that brought the client in for career counseling has faded, and his or her motivation to work has faded as well.

DOCUMENTATION OF TREATMENT PLANS

In an age where client litigation is at the forefront, accurate report writing and record keeping becomes a critical issue. Seligman (1996) says that "the growth and professionalism of the counseling field as well as the increasing emphasis on accountability has led to an expanding need for counselors to document and substantiate the value of their work" (p. 299). Because a great deal of information will be gathered in a fairly short number of sessions, intake interviews and information from additional sessions used for treatment planning must be documented. A sample intake form is provided in Chapter 4.

Record Keeping

Two methods used to remember important information are note taking and tape recording. Each method has its advantages and disadvantages. Note taking is much less threatening than tape recording; however, it can prevent you from giving your full attention to actively listening to your client. In addition, it is virtually impossible to record everything your client says. With note taking, you are bound to miss some information. Note taking can also be distracting to the client.

On the other hand, tape recording may be viewed by your client as an intrusion and may make your client feel uneasy. After the initial shock of being tape-recorded is over, however, tape recording eventually is much less distracting to most clients than note taking. In addition, with tape recording you can preserve as much of the client's information as possible. You must decide which method is best for you to use with your clients.

Progress Notes

Progress notes are another type of record you should keep on each client. Seligman (1996) states that "progress notes are entries made in the client's chart or file each time the counselor has a session or other significant interaction with a client" (p. 316). Progress notes can help the career counselor gauge client progress and plan the direction of treatment, ease the transfer of a client from one counselor to another, and provide a written record should the client return to counseling at a later date.

Progress notes do not have to be structured comments written in the client's record after significant contacts with the career counselor. Having a framework for the writing of progress notes, however, will take less time on your part and make the progress notes more useful. Many different formats are currently available for maintaining progress notes. The SOAP format (Law, Moracco, & Wilmarth, 1981) has been widely adopted in mental health counseling and can be very useful for career counselors to adopt. This format uses the following four categories, which are covered in each progress note:

1. *Subjective:* In this section, the career counselor summarizes his or her impressions of the session. This summarization may include the degree of progress made in the session, the client's affect and mood, interactions between the client and the career counselor, and any other important feelings or thoughts about the information covered in the session.
2. *Objective:* In this section, specific information and facts about the client's progress are documented. Objective information about the client's behavior and the nature of the session is documented.

3. *Analysis:* In this section, the career counselor analyzes the implications of the material identified in the two previous sections. The counselor should be sure to comment on the relationship of that particular session to the client's overall treatment goals.
4. *Plans:* In this section, the career counselor focuses on future plans for the client and lists specific tasks that the client will undertake. Also included in this section are things the counselor will do to prepare for future sessions with the client and areas to be explored in future sessions. Long-range plans for the client are included in this section.

Although there are a variety of other formats that can be used for writing progress notes, you should be consistent in using the format you choose. I believe that the SOAP method is the best for career counselors because it has been widely adopted for use by most community agencies.

 PART TWO

THE INTAKE INTERVIEW

 CHAPTER 4

INFORMATION-GATHERING PROCESS

In career counseling, accurate interviewing and assessment are critical in diagnosing the client's problem and in developing and implementing an effective treatment plan. The intake and information process, or intake interview, is the first important step in the process of career counseling. The intake interview will probably be your first meeting with your client. The process consists of much more than merely gathering background information. This interview is your opportunity to gather comprehensive information about the client so that you can formulate a diagnosis and develop a treatment plan. Intake interviews also help to determine whether you are able to treat the person or whether a referral to another agency is appropriate. In addition, they provide the counselor with an opportunity to explore the client's fears, motivation, and commitment.

Clients entering into career counseling have a unique story to tell that is a combination of who they are, what they have done in the past, how they live, and their career-related problems. Your job as a career counselor, in the initial stage, is to gather information by observing the client and allowing her sufficient time to tell her story. Within the client's story are the keys to helping her enhance her career development. This chapter focuses on using basic career counseling skills to help clients explore information about their significant others, their lifestyle, and the types of career-related problems that bring them to counseling. Included will be some actual dialogue the career counselor can use to help the client tell her story.

THE INTAKE ASSESSMENT

As a career counselor, you need to know as much as possible about your client and the context in which her concerns have occurred. This requires learning all you can about the client and her family background. For career counselors, the intake assessment is usually a two-step process. The first step is to gather information about the client's career development, and the second step is to gather information about the client's personal history and life development. This can be done at the same time in the initial intake assessment session. Information about each of these information-gathering steps is provided in the following text.

Step 1: Gathering Demographic and Career Information

The first part of the intake interview will be comprised of gathering demographic, or identifying, information and career information. This information will include such aspects as:

1. Name and address
2. Gender
3. Date of birth
4. Ethnic and cultural background, native language, and religion
5. Marital and family status
6. Educational level (including all degrees, certifications, seminars, and college information)
   a. Tell me about your educational history.
   b. What are your educational strengths and weaknesses?
   c. What courses did you like best in school?
   d. Have you thought about pursuing additional education?
   e. Which teachers influenced you the most?
   f. What kind of a student have you been?
   g. What types of certificates and certifications have you received and in what subjects?
   h. What are your educational aspirations?
   i. Are you interested in returning to school at this time?
7. Current occupation and employment history (including times of unemployment)
   a. Tell me about your work history.
   b. What types of work do you like?
   c. What types of work do you not like?
   d. For what types of work do you have the most ability?
   e. When in your work history have you been unemployed and for how long?
   f. What types of part-time jobs have you had?
8. Career development information (including influences on the client's career, childhood fantasies, volunteer experiences, limitations, and civic involvement)
   a. What volunteer work experiences have you had?
   b. How do you spend your leisure time?

    c. What were your childhood occupational fantasies?

    d. Do you have any special hobbies that interest you?

    e. Who has had the greatest influence on your career choices?

    f. Do you have any physical limitations, and if so, how have they affected your career development?

    g. What aspects of work have been most satisfying for you?

    h. What aspects of work have been most dissatisfying for you?

9. Career counseling concerns/presenting problem (a brief statement about the person's complaints and troubles, the person's perceptions of why he or she needs career counseling at this time, and what type of help is needed)

    a. What experiences have led you to decide to seek career counseling at this time?

    b. When did you first start to think about seeking career counseling?

    c. What sort of help would you like to have in our career counseling sessions?

    d. What do you think the career counseling experience will be like?

    e. How can career counseling help you?

    f. Have you received career counseling in the past? If so, when and for what reason?

    g. Have you ever had help with career and life planning, and if so, what was the experience like for you?

To gather career information about your client, you will want to use a form similar to that shown in Figure 4.1. Information gathered for the Career/Life Exploration Record will help facilitate the career counseling process. This record should be kept confidential and should not be released to any person without the participant's authorization.

Step 2: Gathering Personal History Information

Because career counseling often involves some personal counseling, career counselors will also want to gather information about the client's life in general. Many agencies have a form on which counselors document their conversation with the client. Other agencies allow the intake interviewer to determine the information that is needed and to write a summary and analysis of the information.

The other components that are part of most intake interviews in career counseling include mental status examination and medical history.

Mental Status Examination. Most mental status examinations can be conceptualized by using the following categories:

Figure 4.1   Sample Intake Form

————

CAREER/LIFE EXPLORATION RECORD

I. IDENTIFYING INFORMATION

Name: _____
　　　　　　　(Last)　　　　　　　　　　(First)　　　　　　　　　　(Middle)

Address: _____
　　　　　　(No.)　　　　(Street)　　　　　(City)　　　　　(State)　　(Zip)

Phone: _____

Referred by: _____

Date of Birth: _____   Sex: Male ☐ Female ☐

Race: White ☐ African American ☐ Asian American ☐

Hispanic American ☐ Native American ☐ Other _____

Marital Status: Single ☐ Married ☐ Separated ☐ Divorced ☐ Widowed ☐

How Long? _____

Spouse's Name: _____   Spouse's Occupation: _____

Children:

Name	Age	Occupation
_____	_____	_____
_____	_____	_____
_____	_____	_____
_____	_____	_____

Father's Occupation: _____   Level of Education: _____

Mother's Occupation: _____   Level of Education: _____

	Name	Age	Education	Occupation	Married?
Sister(s):	_____	____	_____	_____	Yes No
	_____	____	_____	_____	Yes No
	_____	____	_____	_____	Yes No
Brother(s):	_____	____	_____	_____	Yes No
	_____	____	_____	_____	Yes No
	_____	____	_____	_____	Yes No

Figure 4.1 Sample Intake Form (continued)

II. EDUCATION

High School: _____ Year of Graduation: _____

College or Vocational Training: _____

         Degree/Year _____ Major: _____

         Degree/Year _____ Major: _____

         Degree/Year _____ Major: _____

Additional Education (Courses, Seminars, Certification Programs, etc.):

_____

_____

Are you currently in school at this time?   Yes ☐   No ☐

Are you interested in returning to school at this time?   Yes ☐   No ☐

What are your educational aspirations? _____

III. EMPLOYMENT HISTORY

Work Experience: (List the most recent job first and work backward)

       Position   Employer   Time employed

_____

_____

_____

_____

_____

_____

_____

Special hobbies, leisure interests, volunteer work, civic involvement, etc:

_____

_____

_____

_____

_____

Figure 4.1   Sample Intake Form (continued)

IV.   CAREER DEVELOPMENT INFORMATION

What are your present career aspirations? Assume no barriers to achieving them.

_____

_____

_____

_____

Who or what has had the greatest influence on your career choice(s)?

_____

_____

_____

What was your childhood occupational interest or fantasy?

_____

_____

What leisure activities or hobbies do you enjoy now and/or have you enjoyed in the past?

_____

_____

_____

_____

Do you have any physical limitations? (List conditions and their effect on your career development)

_____

_____

_____

What aspects of your work situations have been most satisfying? (i.e., salary, autonomy, coworkers, tasks, responsibility, variety, etc.)

_____

_____

_____

_____

Figure 4.1   Sample Intake Form (continued)

What aspects of your work situations have been most dissatisfying?

_____

_____

_____

_____

V.   CAREER COUNSELING CONCERNS

Please indicate your reason(s) for participating in career counseling

☐   Desire to improve self.

☐   Need assistance in career decision making.

☐   Uncertain about career options.

☐   Leaving the area. Desire to explore relocation and job search strategies.

☐   Need to plan for the future.

☐   Need to alter career goals.

☐   Need assistance in choosing a college major.

☐   Need to set long-range career goals.

☐   Need for occupational information.

☐   Need for labor market information.

☐   Desire to prepare for a position change (i.e., promotion, demotion, transfer).

☐   Job terminating. Desire to explore job search strategies.

☐   Job search assistance.

☐   Career stress.

☐   Job dissatisfaction due to working conditions (i.e., work hours, place of work).

☐   Job dissatisfaction due to job duty requirements.

☐   Job dissatisfaction due to interpersonal relations with peers or supervisor.

☐   General life dissatisfaction.

☐   Relationship pressures (spouse, parents, children, significant others, peers, etc.)

1. Appearance
    a. General impressions
    b. Nature and appropriateness of clothing
    c. Cleanliness
    d. Unusual physical characteristics
2. Behavior
    a. Attitude toward counselor (eye contact, willingness to respond to questions, etc.)
    b. Habits (smoking, rocking, etc.)
    c. Movement retardation or agitation
    d. Tremors or tics
    e. Apparent disabilities (visual, motor, auditory)
    f. Other unusual mannerisms
3. Speech
    a. Articulation or communications difficulties
    b. Speech pressured or slowed
    c. Unusual or idiosyncratic speech or word usage
4. Emotions
    a. Observable emotions, including affect and immediate as well as underlying, long-standing emotional states
    b. Range of emotions exhibited
    c. Appropriateness of emotions
    d. Lability of mood
    e. Flat or blunted affect
5. Orientation to reality
    a. Awareness of time (hour, month, day, and year)
    b. Awareness of place (where the interview is being conducted)
    c. Awareness of persons (who counselor and client are)
    d. Awareness of situation (what is presently going on)
6. Concentration and attention
    a. Ability to focus on stimuli (ask client to repeat three words in reverse order or to repeat at least five digits)
    b. Ability to sustain attention (ask client to subtract 7s from 100)
    c. Alert and responsive (or lethargic and/or distracted)
7. Thought processes
    a. Capacity for abstract thinking
    b. Flight of ideas
    c. Loose associations
    d. Repetitions or perseverations
    e. Coherence and continuity of thoughts
    f. Responses delayed or confused
8. Thought content
    a. Suicidal ideation
    b. Violence or aggression

   c. Delusions
   d. Obsessions or compulsions
   e. Fears or phobias
   f. Ideas of persecution
   g. Other prominent thoughts
9. Perception
   a. Hallucinations (list type)
   b. Other unusual sensory experiences
10. Memory
   a. Adequacy of immediate memory (check immediate recall)
   b. Adequacy of short-term memory (check recall of information provided earlier in the interview)
   c. Adequacy of long-term memory (check recall of information from last few days, weeks, or months)
11. Intelligence
   a. Educational level
   b. Level of vocabulary
   c. Overall intelligence
12. Judgment and insight
   a. Decision-making ability
   b. Problem-solving abilities
   c. Awareness of the nature of his or her problems
   d. Impulsivity
   e. Nature of self-image (especially strengths and weaknesses)

Medical History. The career counselor should identify any past or current illnesses the client has experienced and discuss any medications or medical treatments the person has received:

1. What past or present illnesses and accidents of significance has the person experienced? How has this affected the client's career development and decision making?
2. Describe the nature of any hospitalizations of the client.
3. What past or present medical treatments has the person received?

Some career counselors may not be adequately trained to perform an evaluation in all of the areas discussed here. If you feel that you are not prepared to handle information from any of these categories, you should use this information as a guide for referring your clients to other mental health professionals. In addition, many texts (c.f., Maxmen & Ward, 1995; Seligman, 1996) are available as references for further information about gathering personal and mental health information in an intake interview.

 **CHAPTER 5**

DEVELOPING RAPPORT WITH THE CLIENT

INTERVIEW SKILLS USED IN THE INTAKE ASSESSMENT

A comprehensive interview is required to effectively gain critical information about your clients and their problems. Your counseling skills in general play a big role in information gathering in the initial and subsequent sessions. You must be able to elicit the entire story from your clients. You must be prepared to probe for all relevant information and adequately evaluate and respond to your clients' feelings. Effective interviewing skills will be a critical component in your practice of career counseling. Following is a review of the basic, core counseling skills you will be using as you help clients to tell their story.

Develop Rapport with the Client

As in any type of counseling relationship, it is critical to develop rapport with the client as quickly as possible. Remember that clients typically have a limited time frame in which they can attend career counseling sessions. You must be able to build enough trust in clients so that they feel free to discuss their career concerns and related issues in a relatively short period of time. Most clients tend to feel very nervous and uncertain in the early stages of counseling. The majority do not know what to expect from the career counseling sessions. Thus, part of your job is to ensure that clients feel comfortable and safe in disclosing information about themselves and their lives.

Career counseling is often viewed as simply helping clients to assess themselves, providing them with information about the world-of-work, and then matching clients with the most appropriate jobs available. Other times career counseling is seen as the process of guiding people through the selection of an occupation. Both of these views hold career counseling as an impersonal relationship that is educational in nature. In actuality, the process is very interpersonal and requires some type of relationship between the career counselor and the client. In career counseling, there is typically an interrelationship between the clients' career problems and their personal problems. Career counselors are often required to work in both areas when working with their clients. Therefore, the relationship between you and your clients is critical in the career counseling process.

Many things you do will help to build rapport between you and the client. For example, "small talk" can be used to help clients feel more at ease and less anxious about starting the career counseling process. This talk can be about anything that comes into your mind as you meet each client for the first time. Career counselors should also use the client's name as much as possible without overdoing it. In addition, the client may be asked what she would like to be called in case she has a special nickname, although this brings up a boundary issue. Many counselors believe that it is more appropriate to use formal titles when addressing the client (Mr., Ms., Mrs. Green) and expect the client to use the counselor's title when addressing them. My personal belief is that career counseling is a mutual process, and I prefer that my clients call me by my first name. Some counselors would say that this breaks the boundary between client and therapist, but I believe that the trade-off in rapport development makes it worthwhile. You must make your own determination about how you react to this issue with your clients.

The career counselor stresses that he and the client are in this career counseling process together. The career counselor also will describe what the client should express and should address the client's fears in the initial session. Additionally, in the intake interview, it is important to explain the career counseling process, establish "rules" for future sessions, and present your qualifications and the services that you offer. All these things will enhance the rapport between the counselor and client and make the process seem less ambiguous.

COUNSELOR: Hello. How are you today, Kathy?

CLIENT: I'm fine. How are you, Dr. Jones?

COUNSELOR: Please call me John. I'm great! Except for the weather. I tried to do a little yard work this weekend, but it rained too much.

CLIENT: That's for sure! I didn't go anywhere.

COUNSELOR: I know what you mean, Kathy. Is Kathy what you would like me to call you?

CLIENT: Yes!

COUNSELOR: I would like to spend some time now talking about the career counseling process we are about to undertake. I will tell you about the kinds of things you should expect from me and the kinds of things I will expect of you. Hopefully this will address any concerns or fears you have about career counseling.

At this point in the initial interview, the career counselor is merely starting to develop rapport with the client and make her feel more at ease. The counselor tries to communicate a sincere desire to get to know the client. In addition, the counselor attempts to ease the client's anxiety about the career counseling process. Many clients come for career counseling with a set of unrealistic expectations and fears about what will happen during the sessions to come.

Observe and Attend to the Client

Your primary responsibility is to attend to your client and really listen to what your client is saying. You need to help your client talk freely about his career concerns. Observation can be one of the most valuable tools for you to use in gathering information about your clients. During each session with your clients, you need to be aware of clues that may affect the outcome of the career counseling sessions.

Attending means that you are listening very closely to what the client is telling you. It means listening not only to the words but also to the hidden messages behind the words. It means observing body language, observing the client's affect while he is talking with you, and noting his general mood while he is in your office. You should observe his general appearance and note any clues about the client's grooming, posture, and mannerisms. You should observe how much the client talks and how much he discloses about himself. Resistant clients will present themselves in such a way as to indicate that they are not really interested in your help; they may have been referred by someone or some other agency and are simply fulfilling legal obligations. You should maintain eye contact with the client as a way of showing interest in him and in his concerns. Sustained eye contact, however, is considered to be offensive in some cultures. Judge each client on an individual basis. You should also note if the client maintains eye contact with you. This may give you information about the current level of self-esteem. Observe the client's facial expressions and his affect as he begins to tell you his story.

Another important element in attending to the client is your posture. The way you sit when you talk with the client says a lot about your interest in the client. Most of the time, sitting so that you lean forward toward the client in a relaxed manner is recommended. You should, however, be cognizant of clients from other cultures. Some clients may feel uncomfortable if you are sitting too close and "invading their space."

The objective with attending behavior is to encourage the client to verbalize her career-related concerns. In order to do so, she must feel relaxed. Attending allows her to feel safe in disclosing intimate details about herself and her life. I believe it helps clients to explain to you why they are coming to you for career counseling and allow them to "tell their story" before bombarding them with questions. You may also want to jot down some of your impressions about the client and her behavior.

Ask Pertinent Questions

Questions allow you to gather additional information about the client. Open-ended questions are ones that cannot be answered with a yes-no response or in a few words. These types of questions force the client to provide you with maximum information. Open-ended questions typically begin with *how, what,* or *why.* Closed-ended questions are those that simply require a yes-no response or can be answered in a few words. They tend to focus the interview and begin with *are, is,* or *do.* A combination of both types of questions is recommended for an effective initial interview.

━━━━━━ *Intake with Kathy* ━━━━━━

The following notes were made by the career counselor during the initial intake session with Kathy.

Step 1: Gather Demographic and Career Information

COUNSELOR: Kathy, I'm going to be asking you some questions so that we can get an idea about your concerns. Getting an accurate picture of what's going on is important in developing goals to work on in our counseling sessions. Your feedback is very important!

CLIENT: O.k.

COUNSELOR: Now, what sort of help would you like to have from me, Kathy?

CLIENT: I'm not happy in my current job, but I'm not sure what type of job would be best for me.

COUNSELOR: What made you decide on career counseling at this point in your life, Kathy?

CLIENT: I don't know. At first I thought I could deal with it, but I'm quickly becoming more dissatisfied at work. I hate getting up to go to work on Monday mornings.

COUNSELOR: What do you hope to get from career counseling?

CLIENT: I need to find the type of job I'm best suited for.

COUNSELOR: What do you think the career counseling experience will be like?

CLIENT: I think you'll gather information about me and then help me pick out a job that I'm suited for.

Upon being questioned about why the client is seeking career counseling, it becomes apparent that she is undecided about an appropriate career choice. It is also apparent that she has many misconceptions about the career counseling process. She thinks the career counselor's job is to magically match her up with the perfect job for her. She is not taking much responsibility for the process. Many clients in career counseling have this perception of the process. A client such as this one often needs more information about the career counseling process.

COUNSELOR: Kathy . . . have you ever received career counseling in the past?

CLIENT: No, I haven't.

COUNSELOR: Kathy, the career counseling process is much more than giving you a few tests and telling you what type of job is best for you. You are going to have to do a lot of work in these sessions. There will probably be homework assignments as we proceed through counseling, and you will have to do a lot of self-introspection and exploration of the world-of-work. Are you prepared at this time to commit to this work?

CLIENT: I didn't realize that the sessions would be like that, but I'm committed to do what it takes to identify a job that's a better match for me.

Using the Career/Life Exploration Record in Chapter 4 (Figure 4.1), or a similar form, the counselor begins his interview with Kathy by gathering some current demographic information. He notes her sex and ethnicity and then begins:

COUNSELOR: How old are you now, Kathy? (closed-ended demographic question)

CLIENT: 41.

COUNSELOR: Are you currently married? (closed-ended question to determine marital and family status)

CLIENT: Yes, I'm married and have one child, Renee.

COUNSELOR: Tell me about your husband. (open-ended question for additional information)

CLIENT: My husband's name is Kerry. We've been married for about eleven years now. He works as a manager at a local supermarket. (The career counselor will gather more information about Kerry at a later time in the process.)

COUNSELOR: Now tell me about Renee.

CLIENT: Renee is ten years old now. She goes to elementary school. She's the apple of my eye . . . what can I say?

At this point the career counselor has gathered all the demographic information that is necessary to continue with counseling. At a later point in the career counseling process, he will ask Kathy to complete a career genogram to gather more specific information about Kathy's family. The career counselor now proceeds to gather career information from Kathy.

COUNSELOR: Let's talk now about your past work experiences. (open-ended question about work)

CLIENT: Well, I grew up in a very traditional family. I was never exposed to many occupational fields. Women in my family were encouraged to go into career fields like nursing, social work, and teaching. So, a career in one of these fields made sense at the time. I have always enjoyed working with kids and being a role model for young people. I felt like teaching would provide an excellent way for me to do so. So I went to a small college and earned a teaching degree that would allow me to work in elementary and middle schools. I have worked as a teacher for the past six years. Four of those years were in an elementary school and the last two in a middle school.

COUNSELOR: What do you dislike about your current job?

CLIENT: After Kerry and I got married we moved to a large metropolitan area where he was transferred. I got a job in a large middle school. My experience there has not been as positive as my first four years.

COUNSELOR: What is different?

CLIENT: I feel unappreciated and unsupported by the administration. I have also had trouble with the students. I feel like they take advantage of me and I cannot maintain classroom discipline. The students just don't listen to me. When I try to take a stronger stand, I feel like the principal doesn't support me. The students also seem apathetic about learning. I just don't get respect from anyone! I have been able to keep this up for about four years . . . but all the time I have thought about quitting. As summer would come around, I would get reenergized and convince myself that things would get better. But when things didn't get better, I felt like it was time to change.

COUNSELOR: What do you like about teaching?

CLIENT: I feel that my strength is my communication skills. I believe that I speak and write very well. I always liked teaching concepts and working with students on an individual basis. Being a mentor was especially rewarding.

COUNSELOR: What types of other employment or part-time work have you had? (open-ended question to find out more about Kathy's interests)

CLIENT: I worked at the Dairy Queen for two semesters while I was in college, and I worked as a clerk in a supermarket for about nine months.

The career counselor would continue to gather information about likes and dislikes Kathy had from each of the jobs she has had. He then switches to questions about Kathy's educational level.

COUNSELOR: Tell me about your educational history. (open-ended question)

CLIENT: There's not much to tell . . . I graduated from a small high school in the Pittsburgh area and went to a small college where I got a bachelor's degree in Elementary and Middle Childhood Education.

COUNSELOR: What kind of a student have you been?

CLIENT: I am a good student. I graduated with a 3.50 GPA. I was in a lot of clubs and enjoyed many social activities.

COUNSELOR: What courses did you like the best? (closed-ended question)

Notice that the career counselor used a combination of closed-ended and open-ended questions to gather information. Also note that the career counselor skipped any questions dealing with Kathy's family. He will gather information about her parents and siblings using a career genogram later in the interview.

Step 2: Personal Information

Appearance
Tall and thin white female in her 30s. Well-dressed and well-groomed. Wearing neatly pressed slacks and a sweatshirt with a Pittsburgh Steelers logo. Appearance was appropriate for this situation.

Behavior
Kathy appeared nervous and somewhat reluctant. She sat with her legs crossed and wrenched her hands a bit. She appeared fidgety and rocked some in her chair. She maintained good eye contact.

Speech
She spoke in a soft voice, but spoke very slowly and with great effort. Kathy was very articulate in describing her current situation. She was somewhat monotone and deliberate in her speech.

Emotions
Depressed mood off and on for the past year. Her affect appears to be predominantly sad.

Orientation to Reality
Accurately able to describe time, place, and person.

Concentration and Attention
Good concentration, but had some lack of attention.

Thought Processes
Thoughts were logical, but she tends to give too much detail at times. She also seems to drift from the point occasionally.

Thought Content
No disturbances in the way she thought, how she put ideas together, or in the relevance of her thoughts.

Perception
There were no distortions in the way the client perceived reality through any of her senses.

Memory
There were no inconsistencies in the client's immediate, recent, or remote memory.

Intelligence
Intelligence is average to above average. She appeared to have the capacity to learn, understand, and apply knowledge.

Judgment and Insight
Good judgment, seems to understand the consequences of her behavior and its affect on others. Insight was good. She appears to realize she needs some career counseling and is willing to work toward realistic goals.

Medical History
Client states she has been in good health until recently when she has felt a little depressed. No record of other counseling or hospitalizations. Reports some problems with sleeping and eating. No other significant illnesses.

Reflect Client's Feelings

Reflection is a way of expressing to clients that you understand their experience and deep concerns, and that you are trying to perceive the world through their eyes (Brammer, 1979). Reflection involves expressing back to the clients, using different words, their essential feelings. The career counselor would focus not on the content as much as the feelings behind the words.

COUNSELOR: Kathy, you feel like you are undervalued in your job and that you get no respect from your students or the administration.

CLIENT: Yes. They just don't care about me.

COUNSELOR: But I also feel like you feel you cannot quit your job.

CLIENT: I'm not sure we can make it on one salary at this time.

COUNSELOR: You feel frustrated and angry.

Notice that the career counselor picks up on Kathy's frustration and anger. These reflections are gut-level feelings about how the client is really feeling. These feelings are then presented back to the client for accuracy. The counselor's attitude is empathetic, nonjudgmental, and respectful of the client. This helps to foster rapport and a good working relationship.

Paraphrase the Client's Words

Brammer (1979) suggests that paraphrasing has several purposes: (1) testing your understanding of what the client has said; (2) communicating that you are trying to understand the basic message being conveyed; and (3) showing that you have followed the client's verbalizations. He concludes that paraphrasing is "a method of restating the helpee's basic message in similar, but usually fewer, words" (p. 71).

Paraphrasing can be useful in clarifying messages verbalized by the client that you do not understand. Similarly, it can be used to help clients clarify for themselves things they have said. Paraphrasing is also very useful in uncovering feelings that maybe hidden in the client's statements. The counselor generally restates the client's words in a clearer form. Paraphrasing usually takes the form of "What I hear you saying is . . ." or "In other words. . . ." Paraphrases usually communicate to the client that you understand him or her and that you have empathy for the situation. Paraphrasing should be a simple, concise summary of the basic message transmitted by the client.

Use Encouragers

Encouragers are used to get the client to continue talking. Ivey (1994) says that "encouragers have been defined as head nods, open gestures, and positive facial expressions that encourage the client to keep talking" (p. 103). He says the primary encouragers include minimum verbal utterances such as "Ummm" and "Uh-huh"; silence, accompanied by appropriate nonverbal communication; and restatement and repetition of key words.

Clarify Mixed Messages

Clarifying helps clients to make sense out of their verbalizations. Many of the messages clients share with you will be confusing and vague. You will need more explanation from the client. Clarifications usually take the form of "I'm confused about what you just said; let me see if I heard you correctly" or "I'm not sure what you were saying about your last job; could you give me an example?" Clarifiers, like paraphrases, help you to make sure that the information you are receiving from the client is accurate.

Summarize the Client's Information

Summarization is when the career counselor summarizes a big chunk of information that the client has just provided. It involves tying together into one theme several statements made by the client. Summarization is usually most appropriate at the end of a conversation. Summarization includes the use of paraphrasing; the counselor selects highlights and themes conveyed by the client. The counselor may choose to summarize the counseling process up to that point or summarize the feelings the client has expressed.

COUNSELOR: O.k., Kathy, to summarize, you are unhappy living in a large metropolitan area. You enjoy some aspects of teaching, but dislike other aspects. You feel like you have good oral and written communication skills, but are unable to use them in teaching. You are not sure what type of job you would enjoy but know what your skills are. And at the present time, you and your family need your income to live well. Is that an accurate picture?

Be Self-Reflective

How you feel about your clients can be very important in developing rapport and in assisting your clients in the career exploration process. Therefore, you must constantly reflect on your feelings about each client. Since we, as counselors, are also heavily influenced by our own background and upbringing, inappropriate feelings can hinder our ability to gather the information needed to obtain a clear picture of our client.

Therefore, we need to be very aware of our feelings and the sources of those feelings. We all bring our own baggage to the career counseling sessions. We must continually monitor our own feelings about our clients, what they have done in the past, and the decisions they make. Remember that your goal is to show empathy, not sympathy. Empathy means that you can put yourself in the clients' place and feel what they are feeling or what they have felt. Sympathy, on the other hand, means you feel sorry for the client. My golden rule tends to be if you feel mad, glad, sad, bad, or scared when working with a client, the therapeutic process will be compromised. When this is the case, you should refer the client to another counselor.

 CHAPTER 6

SELF- AND WORLD-OF-WORK ASSESSMENT

Another aspect of the intake interview involves helping clients gather information about themselves and the world-of-work. This type of information can be gathered at the beginning or at any time during the career counseling process. These two types of assessment, however, are being covered here as part of the intake interview.

SELF-ASSESSMENT

When gathering additional information about the client, career counselors can rely on a variety of assessment devices. Seligman (1996) states that assessment tools can be quantitative or qualitative. She says that quantitative assessments tend to yield numerical data and are useful for measuring change; on the other hand, qualitative assessments are more subjective, more ambiguous to interpret, and their results have limited reliability and validity. She concludes that "generally, both qualitative and quantitative approaches to assessment are used with a client to provide a picture that has depth and richness as well as adequate reliability" (p. 88).

QUANTITATIVE ASSESSMENTS

Interest Assessment

The Guide for Occupational Exploration Inventory can be used with high school students and adults. Its scores are derived for each of the twelve GOE interest areas.

Author(s):   J. Michael Farr
Publisher: JIST Works, Inc.
            8902 Otis Avenue
            Indianapolis, IN 46216

Career Occupational Preference System (COPS) measures interests and presents a profile in fourteen areas including Science Professional, Science Skilled, Technology Professional, Technology Skilled, Consumer Economics, Outdoor, Business Professional, Business Skilled, Clerical, Communication, Arts Professional, Arts Skilled, Service Professional, and Service Skilled.

Author(s):   R. Knapp and L. Knapp
Publisher: EDITS
            P.O. Box 7234
            San Diego, CA 92107

Career Exploration Inventory (CEI) uses a developmental format to measure a client's interests in work, leisure, and learning. The CEI measures interests in fifteen clusters including Mechanical, Animal Care, Plants, Physical Sciences, Life Sciences, Artistic, Literary Arts, Social Service, Physical Performing, Personal Service, Persuading/Influencing, Protecting, Leading, Clerical, and Financial Detail.

Author(s):   John Liptak
Publisher: JIST Works, Inc.
            8902 Otis Avenue
            Indianapolis, IN 46216

Kuder General Interest Survey is used with sixth- to twelfth-grade students. It measures broad vocational interest areas including Outdoor, Mechanical, Computational, Scientific, Persuasive, Artistic, Literary, Musical, Social Service, and Clerical.

Author(s):   Frederick Kuder
Publisher: Science Research Associates
            155 N. Wacker Drive
            Chicago, IL 60606

Career Assessment Inventory (CAI) provides scores on six general occupational theme scales, twenty-two basic interest scales, and eighty-nine occupational scales. The CAI also has administrative indices and four nonoccupational scales.

Author(s):   C.B. Johansson
Publisher: National Computer Systems, Inc.
            P.O. Box 1294
            Minneapolis, MN 55440

Self-Directed Search (SDS) is designed to measure Holland's personality types including Realistic, Artistic, Investigative, Social, Enterprising, and Conventional.

Author(s):   John Holland
Publisher: Psychological Assessment Resources
              P.O. Box 998
              Odessa, FL 33556

USES Interest Inventory is used primarily in conjunction with the General Aptitude Test Battery. The interest categories are used in conjunction with the Guide to Occupational Exploration and include Plants and Animals, Artistic, Scientific, Protective, Mechanical, Industrial, Business Retail, Selling, Accommodation, Humanitarian, Leading-Influencing, and Physical Performing.

Author(s):   USES
Publisher: United States Employment Service
              200 Constitution Avenue, N.W.
              Washington, DC 20210

Campbell Interest and Skill Survey (CISS) is designed for use with 15-year-old students and above and includes orientation scales such as Influencing, Organizing, Helping, Creating, Analyzing, Producing, and Adventuring. Basic interest and skill scales are subsets of these orientation scales.

Author(s):   David Campbell
Publisher: National Computer Systems, Inc.
              P.O. Box 1294
              Minneapolis, MN 55440

Strong Interest Inventory (SII) utilizes six general occupational themes based on Holland's theory (realistic, investigative, artistic, social, enterprising, and conventional), twenty-three basic interest scales, 207 occupational scales, and twelve new professional scales.

Author(s):   E. K. Strong, Jr., Jo-Ida Hansen, and Davis P. Campbell
Publisher: Consulting Psychologists Press
              577 College Avenue
              Palo Alto, CA 94306

Values Assessment

Values Scale (VS) measures intrinsic and extrinsic life/career values. It measures traditional values including achievement, aesthetics, altruism, economic returns, prestige, and variety but also includes scales such as ability utilization, advancement, authority, creativity, lifestyle, personal development, physical activity, risk, social interaction, social relations, working conditions, cultural identity, physical prowess, and economic security.

Author(s):   Donald Super and Dorothy Nevill
Publisher: Consulting Psychologists Press
             577 College Avenue
             Palo Alto, CA 94306

Minnesota Importance Questionnaire (MIQ) measures twenty psychological needs and six underlying values related to work satisfaction. The values assessed include achievement, altruism, autonomy, comfort, safety, and status. The needs scales provide scores in such areas as security, social status, compensation, achievement, authority, creativity, and morals.

Author(s):   David Weiss, Rene Davis, and Lloyd Lofquist
Publisher: Vocational Psychology Research
             University of Minnesota
             N620 Elliot Hall
             75 East River Road
             Minneapolis, MN 55455

Work Values Inventory (WVI) measures fifteen extrinsic and intrinsic values important to the world-of-work. The WVI is a forty-five-item test yielding scores in areas such as creativity, aesthetics, altruism, intellectual stimulation, independence, achievement, prestige, management, economic returns, security, surroundings, associates, supervisory relations, variety, and way of life.

Author(s):   Donald Super
Publisher: Consulting Psychologists Press
             577 College Avenue
             Palo Alto, CA 94306

Life Values Inventory (LVI) measures fourteen values including Belonging, Concern for Others, Creativity, Dependability, Responsibility, Prosperity, Health and Activity, Privacy, Scientific Understanding, Spirituality, Loyalty to Family or Group, Achievement, Concern for Environment, and Humility. The LVI helps clients crystallize and prioritize their life values.

Author(s):   R. Kelly Crace and Duane Brown
Publisher: National Computer Systems, Inc.
             P.O. Box 1294
             Minneapolis, MN 55440

Aptitude Assessment

Differential Aptitude Test (DAT) was first published in 1947 for measuring the multiple aptitudes of students. The DAT measures eight aptitudes including Verbal Reasoning, Numerical Reasoning, Abstract Reasoning, Perceptual Speed and Accuracy, Mechanical Reasoning, Space Relations, Spelling, and Language Usage.

Author(s):   G. K. Bennett, H. G. Seashore, and A. G. Wesman
Publisher: The Psychological Corporation
             655 Academic Court
             San Antonio, TX 78204

Armed Services Vocational Aptitude Battery (ASVAB) is used by the military to classify and place recruits to the armed services. The ASVAB consists of ten subsets including General Science, Arithmetic Reasoning, Word Knowledge, Paragraph Comprehension, Numerical Operations, Coding Speed, Auto and Shop Information, Mathematics Knowledge, Mechanical Comprehension, and Electronics Information.

Author(s):   Department of Defense
Publisher: U.S. Military Entrance Processing Command
             2500 Green Bay Road
             North Chicago, IL 60064

General Aptitude Test Battery (GATB) is one of the most widely used multiple aptitude batteries. It was developed by the United States Employment Service and provides a measure of nine aptitudes including Intelligence, Verbal Aptitude, Numerical Aptitude, Spatial Aptitude, Clerical Perception, Form Perception, Motor Coordination, Manual Dexterity, and Finger Dexterity.

Author(s):   USES
Publisher: United States Employment Service
             200 Constitution Avenue, N.W.
             Washington, DC 20210

Personality Assessment

Myers-Briggs Type Indicator (MBTI) is based on Carl Jung's theory of personality types. It suggests that an understanding of personality type can help clients in making a career choice and in dealing with problems and people in life. The MBTI contains four pairs of scales including Extroversion versus Introversion, Sensing versus Intuition, Thinking versus Feeling, and Judgment versus Perception.

Author(s):   Iasbel Briggs Myers and Katherine Briggs
Publisher: Consulting Psychologists Press
             577 College Avenue
             Palo Alto, CA 94306

Sixteen PF is primarily concerned with measuring personality attributes including Warmth, Intelligence, Emotional Stability, Dominance, Impulsivity, Conformity, Boldness, Sensitivity, Suspiciousness, Imagination, Shrewdness, Insecurity, Radicalism, Self-Sufficiency, Self-Discipline, and Tension.

Author(s):   Verne Waller
Publisher: IPAT
1801 Woodfield Drive
Savory, IL 61874

Guilford-Zimmerman Temperament Survey (GZTS) has been used in a variety of settings including educational, vocational, and business. The GZTS measures ten personality traits including General Activity, Restraint, Ascendance, Sociability, Emotional Stability, Objectivity, Friendliness, Thoughtfulness, Personal Relations, and Masculinity.

Author(s):   J. P. Guilford, J. S. Guilford, and W. S. Zimmerman
Publisher: Sheridan Psychological Services, Inc.
Orange, CA 92667

Adjective Checklist is a paper-and-pencil personality inventory containing three hundred adjectives. It measures thirty-seven dimensions of personality including fifteen need scales.

Author(s):   H. G. Gough and A. B. Heilburn
Publisher: Consulting Psychologists Press
577 College Avenue
Palo Alto, CA 94306

Diagnostic Assessment

Salience Inventory (SI) measures the importance of five major life roles including student, worker, homemaker, leisurite, and citizen. Each role is assessed from three perspectives—participation, commitment, and value expectations. It includes 170 behavioral and affective items that are rated on a four-point scale.

Author(s):   Donald Super
Publisher: Consulting Psychologists Press
577 College Avenue
Palo Alto, CA 94306

Career Maturity Inventory (CMI) measures the attitudes and competencies related to variables in the career choice process. The CMI has two sections—an attitude test and a competency test. The attitude test measures attitudes toward decisiveness, involvement, independence, orientation, and compromise. The competency test has five sections: self-appraisal, occupational information, goal selection, planning, and problem solving.

Author(s):   J. O. Crites
Publisher: CTB/McGraw-Hill
2500 Garden Road
Monterey, CA 93940

Adult Career Concerns Inventory (ACCI) is a measure of Super's theory of life stages and includes scales for exploration, establishment, maintenance, and disengagement.

Author(s): Donald Super, Albert Thompson, and Richard Lindeman
Publisher: Consulting Psychologists Press
            577 College Avenue
            Palo Alto, CA 94306

Career Decision Scale (CDS) was developed to provide clients with information about their failure to make career decisions. The CDS yields an estimate of indecision as well as information about the antecedents of indecision. The CDS has two scales: Certainty and Indecision.

Author(s): Samuel Osipow
Publisher: Psychological Assessment Resources
            P.O. Box 998
            Odessa, FL 33566

My Vocational Situation (MVS) provides scores on three scales including Vocational Identity, Occupational Information, and Barriers. It was developed to identify barriers to your clients in the decision-making process. These barriers include lack of information, the identification of environmental and personal barriers to occupational choice, and the potential lack of a vocational identity.

Author(s): John Holland, Denise Daiger, and Paul Power
Publisher: Consulting Psychologists Press
            577 College Avenue
            Palo Alto, CA 94306

Career Beliefs Inventory (CBI) was developed by John Krumboltz to assist clients in the identification of problematic self-perceptions and world views. It is based on Krumboltz's social learning theory of career development.

Author(s): John Krumboltz
Publisher: Consulting Psychologists Press
            577 College Avenue
            Palo Alto, CA 94306

Career Development Inventory (CDI) contains five scales including career planning, career exploration, decision making, world-of-work information, and knowledge of preferred occupational group. The scales are combined to give scores in career development attitudes, career development knowledge and skills, and career orientation. The CDI has forms for both junior and senior high school and college and university students.

Author(s):   Donald Super, Albert Thompson, Richard Lindeman, Jean
Jordaan, & Roger Myers
Publisher: Consulting Psychologists Press
             577 College Avenue
             Palo Alto, CA 94306

Job Search Assessment

Barriers to Employment Success Inventory (BESI) is designed to help
individuals identify their major barriers to obtaining a job or succeeding in
their employment. BESI measures five types of barriers to employment
including Personal and Financial, Emotional and Physical, Career Decision-
Making and Planning, Job Seeking Knowledge, and Training and Education.

Author(s):   John Liptak
Publisher: JIST Works, Inc.
             8902 Otis Avenue
             Indianapolis, IN 46216

Job Search Attitudes Inventory (JSAI) was developed to help individuals
identify self-directed job search attitudes and how these attitudes affect their
search for a job. The JSAI measures four primary attitudes including Luck versus Planning, Uninvolved versus Involved, Help from Others versus Self-
Help, and Passive versus Active.

Author(s):   John Liptak
Publisher: JIST Works, Inc.
             8902 Otis Avenue
             Indianapolis, IN 46216

Leisure/Work Search Inventory (LSI) was developed to measure a person's leisure interests in order to help him or her turn these interests into possible employment opportunities in a full- or part-time job, small business
enterprise, or home-based business.

Author(s):   John Liptak
Publisher: JIST Works, Inc.
             8902 Otis Avenue
             Indianapolis, IN 46216

The assessment process can occur at any point throughout the counseling relationship. Some assessment might occur at the beginning of the
counseling process as a part of the information-gathering stage. Assessment
can also occur during the middle stages of career counseling as the need aris-
es. Suppose, for example, that as you progress through your counseling sessions with a client, you discover she has irrational thinking about the career

decision-making process. You could administer an assessment device to help her explore her thought patterns. Assessments may also be made near the end of the counseling relationship as a method of determining how much progress has been made toward the client's goals.

Assessments are tools used by the career counselor to enhance rapport, establish the goals for counseling, and identify characteristics of the client. The planning and implementation of a test regime should equally involve both the counselor and client. In addition, great lengths should be taken to ensure that the client fully understands the purpose and nature of the assessment process and be aware of how the results will be used.

Because assessment enables career counselors and clients to gain insight and perspectives, enhances exploration, and promotes discussion, it can be a very valuable asset in the counseling relationship. Remember, however, that assessment can also be very threatening to the client. Therefore, select assessment instruments for your clients with care. Seligman (1994) developed a set of questions that counselors should ask themselves before making the decision to use assessment devices:

1. What are the goals of the counseling process?
2. What information is needed to accomplish those goals?
3. Have available sources of information such as the client's own experiences and self-knowledge and previous records and tests been used effectively and fully?
4. Does it seem likely that testing and other forms of assessment can provide important information that is not available from other sources?
5. How should testing be planned and integrated into the counseling process to maximize its benefits?
6. What important questions can be answered by the testing? (p. 103)

Career counselors can use these criteria when deciding whether to use assessment instruments for gathering career information.

QUALITATIVE ASSESSMENTS

Card Sorts

Card sorts are stacks of 3-inch by 5-inch cards that can be used by clients to identify a variety of personal characteristics including skills, values, and interests. Clients are typically asked to sort the cards in stacks based on major headings. (In the interests card sort, for example, cards are sorted into such major headings as "very interested," "of little interest," "no interest," and so on.

Career Autobiography

Autobiographies are an excellent way for career counselors to gather information about their clients. Clients can be asked to start at their birth and write about themselves and their lives. This assignment should include jobs, leisure activities, and family information.

Life Line

Clients are asked to take a blank sheet of paper and draw a horizontal line on it. Beginning at the left end of the line (birth) and proceeding to the right end of the line (present), clients recall important experiences in their life and indicate each experience by putting a dot on the line. I usually ask clients to list work experiences on the top portion of the page and leisure and family experiences on the bottom portion of the page.

Narrative

Cochran (1997) is a proponent of having clients compose a narrative of their life as a way of making meaning. The client actually develops a narrative that contains a plot with a beginning, a middle, and an end that brings closure to the problem.

Success Experiences

This includes a self-analysis of the client's past successful experiences to discover hidden talents.

Early Recollections

Adler (1956) was the first to recognize the importance of early recollections as they relate to the lifestyle of the individual. Watkins and Savickas (1990) used early recollections to identify very rich but often difficult to interpret information about the client.

WORLD-OF-WORK ASSESSMENT

Clients in career counseling need to gather information about the world-of-work before they can make accurate career-related decisions. The following career information classification systems provide career counselors with resources to help their clients systematically explore information about a variety of occupations.

Dictionary of Occupational Titles

The *Dictionary of Occupational Titles (DOT)* was developed by the Department of Labor to classify over 20,000 occupations. The DOT uses a nine-digit code to identify the characteristics that differentiate one occupation from another. The DOT helps people understand the world-of-work, shows the interrelationships that exist in the world-of-work, provides a useful basis for filing career material, and provides a basis for career planning and exploration.

In the DOT, the first three digits indicate each occupation's career group. All occupations are organized into nine broad categories represented by the first digit. These broad categories are as follows:

0/1 Professional, technical, and managerial careers
2   Clerical and sales careers
3   Service careers
4   Agricultural, fishery, forestry, and related careers
5   Processing careers
6   Machine trade careers
7   Bench work careers
8   Structural work careers
9   Miscellaneous careers

Suppose a client is interested in learning more about occupation 191.267-010. In this example, the first category—professional, technical, and managerial careers—is represented with the first digit being either a zero (0) or a one (1). The second digit refers to the division within the category. For the professional, technical, and managerial occupation category, there are the following fifteen divisions:

00/01 Careers in architecture, engineering, and surveying
02   Careers in mathematics and physical sciences
04   Careers in life sciences
05   Careers in social sciences
07   Careers in medicine and health
09   Careers in education
10   Careers in museum, library, and archival sciences
11   Careers in law and jurisprudence
12   Careers in religion and theology
13   Careers in writing
14   Careers in art
15   Careers in entertainment and recreation
16   Careers in administrative specializations
18   Managers and officials, not elsewhere classified
19   Miscellaneous professional, technical, and managerial careers

In our example, 19 would be used to locate occupations in the miscellaneous professional, technical, and managerial careers. Then the third digit used in combination with the first two (191) identifies occupations in the group within the miscellaneous professional, technical, and managerial occupation division.

191 Agents and appraisers, not elsewhere classified
193 Radio operators
194 Sound, film, videotape recording, and reproductions careers
195 Careers in social and welfare work

The middle three digits of the DOT classification number describe each occupation in terms of the job's work requirements with data, people, and things. Each occupation requires a worker, to some extent, to utilize a combination of these types of skills on the job. The functions are listed so that they become progressively more complex as the numbers decrease:

Data (4th digit)	*People (5th digit)*	*Things (6th digit)*
0 Synthesizing	0 Mentoring	0 Setting Up
1 Coordinating	1 Negotiating	1 Precision Work
2 Analyzing	2 Instructing	2 Operating/Controlling
3 Compiling	3 Supervising	3 Driving/Operating
4 Computing	4 Diverting	4 Manipulating
5 Copying	5 Persuading	5 Tending
6 Comparing	6 Speaking/Signaling	6 Feeding/Offbearing
	7 Serving	7 Handling
	8 Taking Instructions/ Helping	

In our example, the middle three digits (267) would relate to an occupation that requires the analyzing of data, speaking/signaling to people, and the handling of things. Therefore, this particular occupation requires a high level of skill in working with data, but a low level of skill in working with people and things.

The last three digits of the code indicate a specific occupation within the occupational group. Therefore, even though a code would have the same first six digits, the last three would differentiate one occupation from another. In our example, 010, the final three digits, represent the occupation of real estate appraiser.

Guide for Occupational Exploration

The *Guide for Occupational Exploration (GOE)* classifies all of the over 20,000 occupations listed in the DOT into twelve interest areas, sixty-six work groups, and into subgroups that comprise each work group. The twelve inter-est areas that comprise the GOE are assigned a two-digit code as follows:

01 Artistic—Interest in creative expression of feelings or ideas
02 Scientific—Interest in discovering, collecting, and analyzing infor-mation about the natural world and in applying scientific research findings to problems in medicine, life sciences, and nat-ural sciences
03 Plants and Animals—Interest in activities involving plants and ani-mals, usually in an outdoor setting
04 Protective—Interest in the use of authority to protect people and property
05 Mechanical—Interest in applying mechanical principles to practical situations and in using machines, hand tools, or techniques
06 Industrial—Interest in repetitive, concrete, organized activities in a factory setting
07 Business Detail—Interest in organized, clearly defined activities requiring accuracy and attention to detail, primarily in an office setting
08 Selling—Interest in bringing others to a point of view through per-sonal persuasion, using sales and promotion techniques
09 Accommodating—Interest in catering to the wishes of others, usu-ally on a one-to-one basis
10 Humanitarian—Interest in helping others with their mental, spiritu-al, social, physical, or vocational needs
11 Leading-Influencing—Interest in leading and influencing others through activities involving high-level verbal or numerical abilities
12 Physical Performing—Interest in physical activities performed before an audience

These twelve areas are then divided into sixty-six work groups. For example, 01 Artistic is divided into the following work groups:

01.01 Literary Arts
01.02 Visual Arts
01.03 Performing Arts: Drama
01.04 Performing Arts: Music
01.05 Performing Arts: Dance
01.06 Craft Arts
01.07 Elemental Arts
01.08 Modeling

Because many of the work groups include many occupations, these work groups are then divided into subgroups. For example, 01.01 Literary Arts is divided into the following subgroups:

01.01-01 Editing
01.01-02 Creative Writing
01.01-03 Commercial Art

Standard Industrial Classification

The Standard Industrial Classification (SIC) allows your client to explore occupations by first examining information in a variety of industries. Using the SIC manual, occupations are classified by industry, and industries are grouped based on the activities in which their workers engage. The client first identifies the field in which he is interested in gathering information:

1. Agriculture, forestry, and fisheries
2. Mining
3. Construction
4. Manufacturing
5. Transportation, communications, electric, gas, and sanitary services
6. Wholesale trade
7. Retail trade
8. Finance, insurance, and real estate
9. Services
10. Public administration
11. Nonclassifiable establishments

Then, using the SIC manual, the client explores information about occupations contained within that particular field.

Standard Occupational Classification (SOC)

The Standard Occupational Classification (SOC) system arranges careers into twenty-two divisions. A sample of the divisions includes:

Natural scientists and mathematicians
Teachers, librarians, and counselors
Health technologists and technicians

Each division is then broken into major groups, minor groups, and unit groups. Although this system is complicated, it allows clients to specify occupations of interest within major work groups.

Occupational Outlook Handbook (OOH)

The *Occupational Outlook Handbook (OOH)* was developed by the United States Bureau of Labor Statistics, United States Department of Labor, and presents occupations by career families. For each occupation, the OOH provides information about job duties, working conditions, level and places of employment, education and training requirements, job employment outlook, advancement possibilities, earnings, and related occupations. The occupations are grouped according to the SOC manual, but the OOH also contains an index referenced to the most recent edition of the *Dictionary of Occupational Titles (DOT)*.

The OOH answers many of the general questions clients will ask about occupations of interest to them. Whether a client is preparing to enter the world-of-work, is changing occupations, or is re-entering the labor force after an absence, the OOH can be a highly informative resource. The *Occupational Outlook Quarterly (OOQ)* is published by the Department of Labor to keep career counselors informed between editions of the OOH.

Occupational Information Network (O*NET)

The Occupational Information Network (O*NET) is a computerized database of information about occupations. The O*NET provides information on approximately 2,000 occupations. The O*NET was not developed as a book but has been published by JIST Works, Inc., as *The O*NET Dictionary of Occupational Titles*. The O*NET was developed to replace an older occupational database that formed the basis of the 1991 version of the *Dictionary of Occupational Titles (DOT)*. It provides information such as a description of the occupation, OOH titles, occupational task list, earnings and education, general work activities, and correlations with other career resources.

Roe's Classification System

In an attempt to study a variety of occupations, Roe developed a two-dimensional classification system (see Table 6.1) based on the primary activities of the occupations included in it. This classification system correlates occupational fields and level of responsibility in occupations. Jobs, therefore, are classified by the type of occupational group and by the responsibility required in the occupation. The two-dimensional system includes eight occupational fields and six levels of occupations.

Eight Occupational Fields.

1. *Service:* Activities involving doing things for other people. Occupations in this group include social workers, counselors, occupational therapists, probation officers, detectives, barbers, police officers, waiters, fire fighters, and hospital attendants.
2. *Business Contact:* Activities involving persuading others, possibly selling products or goods. Occupations in this group include promoters,

public relations personnel, salespeople, auctioneers, interviewers, and buyers.

3. *Organization:* Activities involving management for a government agency or in a private business. Occupations in this group include certified public accountants, employment managers, cashiers, clerks, notaries, and messengers.

4. *Technology:* Activities involving making, producing, and transporting products. Occupations in this group include engineers, electricians, truck drivers, bulldozer operators, and scientists.

5. *Outdoor:* Activities involving the protection of the environment, production of crops and forest products, and working with natural resources. Occupations in this group include landscape architects, farm owners, forest rangers, fish and game wardens, laboratory testers, gardeners, and lumberjacks.

6. *Science:* Activities involving the development and application of natural, physical, and social sciences. Occupations in this group include research scientists, medical specialists, museum curators, pharmacists, veterinarians, chiropractors, and veterinary hospital attendants.

7. *General Culture:* Activities involving the humanities and human culture such as law, ministry, history, and education. Occupations in this group include college professors, editors, elementary and secondary school teachers, radio announcers, reporters, librarians, and law clerks.

8. *Arts and Entertainment:* Activities involving performing for the public or creating in the areas of art, music, writing, and athletics. Occupations in this group include athletes, art critics, designers, music arrangers, interior decorators, advertising artists, illustrators, and photographers.

Six Levels of Occupations.

1. *Professional and Managerial 1:* Responsibilities of these people are important and include independent responsibility and making policy decisions that affect many people. These professions usually require a high level of education, sometimes a doctorate.

2. *Professional and Managerial 2:* People in this category often have less independence and fewer responsibilities. They interpret policy and make decisions for themselves or others. They possess a bachelor's degree, or possibly a master's degree.

3. *Semiprofessional and Small Business:* High school education is required, or maybe technical school or a four-year degree. This category involves a moderate level of responsibility for others.

Table 6.1   Roe's Classification of Occupations

Level	I Service	II Business Contact	III Organization	IV Technology	V Outdoor	VI Science	VII General Cultural	VIII Arts and Entertainment
1	Personal therapists. Social work supervisors. Counselors.	Promoters.	U.S. president and cabinet officer. Industrial tycoon. International bankers.	Inventive geniuses. Consulting or chief engineers. Ship's commanders.	Consulting specialists.	Research scientists. University, college faculties. Medical specialists. Museum curators.	Supreme Court justices. University, college faculties. Prophets. Scholars.	Creative artists, performers (great). Teachers (university equivalent). Museum curators.
2	Social workers. Occupational therapists. Probation, truant officers (with training).	Promoters. Public relations counselors.	Certified public accountants. Business and government executives. Union officials. Brokers (average).	Applied scientists. Factory managers. Ships' officers. Engineers.	Applied scientists. Landowners and operators (large). Landscape architects.	Scientists, semi-independent. Nurses. Pharmacists. Veterinarians.	Editors. Teachers (high school and elementary).	Athletes. Art critics. Designers. Music arrangers.
3	YMCA officials. Detectives, police sergeants. Welfare workers. City inspectors.	Salesmen: auto, bond, insurance. Dealers, retail and wholesale. Confidence men.	Accountants (average). Employment managers. Owners, catering, drycleaning, and so on.	Aviators. Contractors. Foremen (DOT I). Radio operators.	County agents. Farm owners. Forest rangers. Fish, game wardens.	Technicians, medical, X-ray, museum. Weather observers. Chiropractors.	Justices of the peace. Radio announcers. Reporters. Librarians.	Ad writers. Designers. Interior decorators. Showmen.

4	Barbers. Chefs. Practical nurses. Police officers.	Auctioneers. Buyers (DOT I). House canvassers. Interviewers, poll.	Cashiers, clerks, credit, express, and so on. Foremen, warehouse. Salesclerks.	Blacksmiths. Electricians. Foremen (DOT II). Mechanics (average).	Laboratory testers, dairy products, and so on. Miners. Oil well drillers.	Technical assistants.	Law clerks.	Advertising artists. Decorators, window and so on. Photographers. Racing car drivers.
5	Taxi drivers. General house workers. Waiters. City firemen.	Peddlers.	Clerks, file, stock, and so on. Notaries. Runners. Typists.	Bulldozer operators. Delivery people. Smelter workers. Truck drivers.	Gardeners. Farm tenants. Teamsters. Cowpunchers. Miners' helpers.	Veterinary hospital attendants.		Illustrators, greeting cards. Showcard writers. Stagehands.
6	Chambermaids. Hospital attendants. Elevator operators. Watchmen.		Messenger boys.	Helpers. Laborers. Wrappers. Yardmen.	Dairy hands. Farm laborers. Lumberjacks.	Nontechnical helpers in scientific organizations.		

From *The Psychology of Occupations,* by Anne Roe. Copyright © 1956, John Wiley and Sons, Inc.

4. *Skilled:* Training is required, usually an apprenticeship, vocational education, technical school, or high school.
5. *Semiskilled:* On-the-job training or special schooling is required.
6. *Unskilled:* Little training is required and no special education is needed. People in this category only need to be able to follow directions.

This classification system appears to be Roe's greatest contribution. It has been adapted for use in many current assessment instruments. The most prominent of these assessment devices is the Career Occupational Preference System (COPS). The COPS provides scores for each of Roe's groups as well as scales for multiple levels per interest group.

Computerized Guidance Systems

Because information is critical in career decision making, computer-assisted systems for career information and guidance can be very helpful to your clients. Isaacson and Brown (1993) said that these systems can help your client to learn about herself and her psychological world, to learn about the world-of-work, and to expand her options, narrow choices, and make career decisions and career plans. Computers can be used in each of these activities or to supplement other types of exploration activities.

The most commonly used computer-assisted career guidance systems include Career Information System, Guidance Information System, Discover, System of Interactive Guidance and Information (SIGI Plus), and Choices. You should choose a computer-assisted career guidance system based on the quality of information provided to your clients, the sophistication of the technology necessary to operate the system, the user-friendliness of the system, and the management system of the program.

 PART THREE

DEVELOPING TREATMENT PLANS

CHAPTER 7

CONCEPTUALIZING DEVELOPMENTAL THEORIES

Until about 1950, the trait-factor model (Parsons, 1909) was used exclusively by career counselors to "match" clients with appropriate occupations. The focus of career counseling in the early fifties, though, changed to one in which the career and life development of the client became the focal point. In the assessment of today's clients in career counseling, the counselor should begin by looking at the client's career development over the life span. This approach to career counseling forms the first premise of the comprehensive approach to career counseling discussed in Chapter 1: *Career choice is a developmental process that encompasses one's work and one's leisure experiences over a period of time.* This chapter builds upon this premise by showing career counselors how to examine the client's current stage of the life span, roles that the client has played and is currently playing, and the socioeconomic factors that influence career development.

GINZBERG, GINSBURG, AXELRAD, AND HERMA'S DEVELOPMENTAL MODEL

Ginzberg, Ginsburg, Axelrad, and Herma (1951) were the first to abandon the notion of matching clients and occupations as the only way to assist clients in the choice of an occupation. They believed that career counselors must also look at the client's developmental history and the developmental stages in which they are currently functioning. They gave credence to the idea that career behavior is rooted in the early life of the child and develops over time. They were the first to take a holistic look at how people, particularly adolescents, make career decisions.

Ginzberg et al.'s original theory had the following three premises:

1. Decision making is a process that occurs from puberty to the late teens or early 20s.

2. The process of making decisions is largely irreversible.
3. The resolution of the career choice process is a compromise.

Ginzberg et al. (1951) asserted that "occupational choice is a developmental process; it is not a single decision, but a series of decisions made over a period of years. Each step in the process has a meaningful relation to those which precede and follow it" (p. 185). They also believed that the career decision-making process could be divided into three distinct periods or phases:

1. *Fantasy:* Occurs until approximately age 11 and is comprised of the time children spend involved in play. By engaging in a variety of types of play and by playing various roles, children begin to think about the types of work they might like to do in the future.
2. *Tentative:* Children start to make tentative career choices based on information that they gather through various subphases. The tentative phase is comprised of the following subphases:
   a. *Interests (Age 11 or 12):* The individual makes more finite decisions about his or her likes and dislikes.
   b. *Capacity (Age 13 or 14):* The individual becomes aware of his or her abilities as they relate to his or her occupational aspirations.
   c. *Values (Age 15 or 16):* The individual becomes aware of his or her occupational style.
   d. *Transition (Age 17 or 18):* The individual becomes aware of the decision for making a vocational choice.
3. *Realistic:* Adolescents begin to crystallize and specify occupations of interest. The realistic phase is comprised of the following subphases:
   a. *Exploration:* The individual begins to narrow his or her career choices.
   b. *Crystallization:* The individual commits to a specific career field.
   c. *Specification:* The individual selects a job or professional training program.

Ginzberg's model was a drastic change from the trait-factor approaches that were being used for career counseling. The model was the first to elicit information from the client about his or her career/life development and the first to talk about the client going through stages leading to career choice. This model is mainly used for children and adolescents in that it primarily describes the stages that a person goes through up to the end of high school. The next model builds on Ginzberg's notion about career choice being a developmental process in which people pass through clearly defined stages of life and career development. This model, however, also includes stages that an adult might go through over a life span.

Ginzberg (1972) subsequently amended the theory to focus on the contribution of the career choice process across one's life span. His revised theory stated that: (1) occupational choice is a process that remains open as long as one makes and expects to make decisions about work and career; (2) early decisions have a shaping influence on career but so do continuing changes of life and work; and (3) people make decisions with the aim of optimizing satisfaction by finding the best possible fit between their needs and desires and the opportunities and constraints in the world-of-work (p. 173).

Ginzberg (1984) later talked extensively about "occupational choice as a lifelong process of decision-making for those who seek major satisfactions from their work. This leads them to reassess repeatedly how they can improve the fit between their changing goals and the realities of the world of work" (p. 180). He added that the theory predicts that people will make career choices that balance competing interests and values and also take into account the opportunities available and the cost of pursuing the opportunities.

SUPER'S THEORY OF VOCATIONAL DEVELOPMENT

Super's life-span, life-space model of career development is more comprehensive and allows the career counselor to gather more information than the previous model. It is the most extensive theory that describes a person's development over a lifetime. Super (1953) believed that the Ginzberg theory was insufficient in that it did not rely on previous research, did not adequately describe career choice, did not specify what constituted compromise, and was vague about the differences between adjustment and choice.

Super (1953) developed ten propositions that comprised his "theory of vocational development." The propositions focused on human development over the life span by identifying the progression through vocational choice, entry, and adjustment to a vocation. The original ten propositions have since been expanded and revised to incorporate new thinking about occupations and to take into account new changes in our society (Super, 1981, 1985, 1990; Super & Bachrach, 1957). Super's life-span, life-space theory of career development is now comprised of fourteen propositions, which are described in the following text.

Proposition 1. People differ in their abilities and personalities, needs, values, interests, traits, and self-concepts.

Proposition 2. Each person is qualified, by virtue of these characteristics, for a number of occupations.

Proposition 3. Each occupation requires a characteristic pattern of abilities and personality traits, with tolerances wide enough to allow some variety of occupations for each individual as well as some variety of individuals in each occupation.

Proposition 4. Vocational preferences and competencies, the situation in which people live and work, and hence their self-concepts change with time and experience, although self-concepts as products of social learning are increasingly stable from late adolescence until late maturity, providing some continuity in choice and adjustment.

Proposition 5. This process of change may be summed up in a series of life stages (a "maxi-cycle") characterized as a sequence of growth, exploration, establishment, maintenance, and disengagement; and these stages may, in turn, be subdivided into periods characterized by developmental tasks. A small (mini) cycle takes place during career transitions from one stage to the next or each time an individual's career is destabilized by illness or injury, employer's reduction in force, social changes in human resource needs, or other socioeconomic or personal events. Such unstable or multiple-trial careers involve recycling of new growth, reexploration, and reestablishment (recycling).

Proposition 6. The nature of the career pattern—that is, the occupational level attained and the sequence, frequency, and duration of trial and stable jobs—is determined by the individual's parental socioeconomic level, mental ability, education, skills, personality characteristics (needs, values, interests, and self-concepts), and career maturity and by the opportunities to which he or she is exposed.

Proposition 7. Success in coping with the demands of the environment and of the organism in that context at any given life-career stage depends on the readiness of the individual to cope with these demands—that is, on his or her career maturity.

Proposition 8. Career maturity is a hypothetical construct. It is a psychosocial construct that denotes an individual's degree of vocational development along the continuum of life stages and substages from growth through disengagement. From a social or societal perspective, career maturity can be operationally defined by comparing the developmental tasks being encountered to those expected based on the individual's chronological age. From a psychological perspective, career maturity can be operationally defined by comparing an individual's resources, both cognitive and affective, for coping with a current task to the resources needed to master that task.

Proposition 9. Development through the life stages can be guided in part by facilitating the maturing of abilities, interests, and coping resources and in part by aiding in reality testing and in the development of self-concepts.

Proposition 10. The process of career development is essentially that of developing and implementing occupational self-concepts. It is a synthesizing and compromising process in which the self-concept is a product of the interaction of inherited aptitudes, physical makeup, opportunity to observe and play various roles, and evaluations of the extent to which the results of role-playing meet with the approval of supervisors and peers (interactive learning).

Proposition 11. The process of synthesis or compromise between individual and social factors, between self-concepts and reality, is one of role-playing and of learning from feedback, whether the role is played in fantasy, in the counseling interview, or in such real-life activities as classes, clubs, part-time work, and entry jobs.

Proposition 12. Work satisfactions and life satisfactions depend on the extent to which an individual finds adequate outlets for abilities, needs, values, interests, personality traits, and self-concepts. Satisfactions depend on establishment in a type of work, a work situation, and a way of life in which one can play the kind of role that growth and exploratory experiences have led one to consider congenial and appropriate.

Proposition 13. The degree of satisfaction people attain from work is proportional to the degree to which they have been able to implement self-concepts.

Proposition 14. Work and occupation provide a focus for personality organization for most men and women, although for some individuals this focus is peripheral, incidental, or even nonexistent. Then other foci, such as leisure activities and homemaking, may be central. Social traditions   such as sex-role stereotyping and modeling, racial and ethnic biases, and the opportunity structure—as well as individual differences are important determinants of preferences for such roles as worker, student, leisurite, homemaker, and citizen.

Developmental Stages of the Life Span

Super (1990) believed that people pass through five developmental stages over a lifetime. These five life stages influence a person's career development and career choices. Much of Super's life-span theory was developed from his research on psychosocial life-stage theorists. Super (1980) summarized the life stages and the tasks of each stage as follows.

*1. Physical and Psychological **Growth** (0–14 Years).* During this stage, a self-concept develops through the identification of activities taking place at home and at school. Needs and fantasy dominate this growth stage, and interest and capacity become increasingly important as a person increases his or her social participation and does reality testing. Substages of the growth stage include:

> *Fantasy (4–10 Years):* Needs remain dominant aspects of the person's life, and role-playing in fantasy takes place.
>
> *Interest (11–12 Years):* Likes are the major determinant of the person's aspirations and activities. The person avoids activities that are not interesting.
>
> *Capacity (13–14 Years):* Abilities take precedence in life, and the person begins to consider a variety of career requirements including training and salary.

2. Exploration (15–24 Years). During this stage, self-examination, role experimentation, and occupational exploration take place in part-time jobs, leisure activities, and school activities. Substages of the exploration stage include:

Tentative (15–17 Years): The person considers his or her interests, needs, capacities, values, and opportunities in making tentative choices about a variety of occupations. These tentative choices are then tried out in course work, hobbies, fantasy, volunteering, and full- or part-time jobs.

Transition (18–21 Years): The person enters either the world-of-work or professional training and attempts to implement a self-concept. At this point, reality considerations are given precedence.

Trial—Little Commitment (22–24 Years): After identifying an appropriate field, the first work role in it is found and tried out as a potential for life work.

3. Establishment in an Occupation (25–44 Years). During this stage, the person has identified an appropriate field in which to work and makes an effort to establish a permanent place in that field. Establishment may begin with or without trial early in this stage. Substages of the establishment stage include:

Trial—Commitment and Stabilization (25–30 Years): The field of work presumed to be suitable may prove unsatisfactory, resulting in one or two changes before the person's life work is found or before it becomes clear that the person's life work will be a series of unrelated career activities.

Advancement (31–44 Years): As the person's career pattern becomes clear, effort is made to stabilize and make a secure place in the world-of-work. This substage is when the person tends to be most creative.

4. Maintenance of Work Situation (45–64 Years). During this stage, the person is most concerned with holding onto work. Emphasis is placed on maintaining satisfying aspects of work, while revising unsatisfying aspects of work.

5. Disengagement from Work (65+ Years). During this stage, the person sees a decline in physical and mental powers. The person experiences a decline in work hours, and new roles replace the work role. Substages of the disengagement stage include:

Deceleration (65–70 Years): The pace of the person's work slackens, and duties may be shifted or altered to suit declining capacities. Many people find part-time work to replace their full-time jobs.

Retirement (71+ Years): The person leaves work and increases use of leisure and other life roles.

These five stages illustrate the ideal career development for an individual. However, career development rarely, if ever, takes this form. Factors that cause a client's career from developing normally include such things as changes in her career path, stopping work to raise children, layoff due to technology, corporate restructuring, downsizing, and spouse relocation. For Kathy, even though chronologically she should be in the establishment stage, she is still in the tentative substage of the exploration stage. In other words, she is still considering her interests, values, and personality characteristics and is ready to explore her occupational options.

Life Space

Super (1990) suggested that your client's career rainbow consists of the constellation of social positions occupied and roles currently being played by your client. Super recommends the career rainbow as a means of helping people to look at the number and variety of roles in which they are currently engaging (see Figure 7.1). In looking at the life roles of the client, it is important to look both at her current roles and at the roles in which she envisions herself engaging in the future. This will give you valuable information about the person's priorities, values, and goals.

Figure 7.1   Super's Career Rainbow

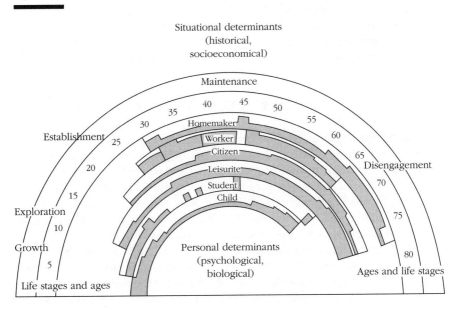

Super and Harris-Bowlsbey (1979) identified the following roles played by most people at some time in their lives:

Student: The time and energy spent in education or training at any time in your life

Citizen: The time and energy spent in civic, school, church, or political activities

Child: Your relationship to your parents or guardians and the time and energy spent in it

Leisurite: The time and energy spent in leisure activity

Homemaker: The time and energy spent in taking responsibility for home maintenance and management

Worker: The time and energy spent in working for pay at any time in your life.

Annuitant: The role that replaces worker; that is, the time in your life when you will receive social security, pension, or other types of retirement income

Spouse: Your relationship with your husband or wife and the time and energy spent in it

Parent: Your relationship with your children and the time and energy spent in it (p. 13)

Career and Life Satisfaction

Super (1990) believed that in counseling clients from the developmental point of view, career counselors need to: (1) develop and accept an integrated picture of clients and their roles; (2) test this concept against reality; and (3) convert it into reality by helping clients make choices that implement the self-concept and lead to job success and satisfaction.

SOCIOECONOMIC THEORY

Social and economic factors have a major influence on a person's career development. These events include national and international events such as increased technology in some industry sectors and plant closings in the United States to move operations to foreign countries. Similarly, events in the client's own state or neighborhood may play a role in her career development. Other people also have an impact on the client's career development. The opinions of peers, neighbors, and family affect one's choice of a career path.

The status attainment theory (Blau & Duncan, 1967) attempts to explain occupational attainment based on the social status of one's parents (see Figure 7.2). According to this theory, the status level of the client's parents affects the level of schooling achieved by the client, thus affecting the occupational

Figure 7.2 **Status attainment theory**

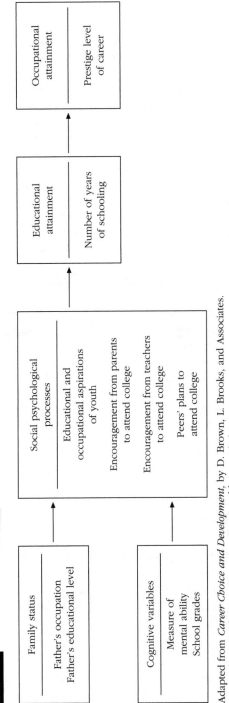

Adapted from *Career Choice and Development,* by D. Brown, L. Brooks, and Associates. Copyright © 1984, Jossey-Bass, Inc. Reprinted by permission.

level the client can achieve. Other researchers (c.f., Clarridge, Sheehy, & Hauser, 1977; Sewell, Haller, & Portes, 1969) have found that both family status and mental ability are predictors of occupational achievement through the influence of educational level, peers and significant others, and career plans.

In the status attainment theory, the social context in which a person develops is crucial to a person's career development and the choices he/she makes. Socioeconomic theories emphasize factors outside the control of the individual such as employment opportunities, parent's occupation, chance or luck, and the economy. The socioeconomic status of the household in which clients are raised affects their career choices. Socioeconomic status includes such factors as parents' income level, educational background, and status in the community; where the parents live; economic conditions; and exposure to educational opportunities and occupational information.

Hotchkiss and Borow (1990) believe that socioeconomic theories focus on why and how certain occupations and occupational perceptions are passed down from generation to generation. They also focus on how socioeconomic factors such as race, gender, parents' occupations, parents' educational status, community, peer pressures, ethnicity, and religion affect the occupational choices of our clients.

McDaniels and Gysbers (1992) believe that in many cases, people base many of their career choices on what they have learned from their environments. They also say that people make vocational and educational decisions based on the options that are available to them.

It is important to explore the client's social and economic factors and how they have affected the person's career development. The counselor will want the client to explore not only his or her commitment to career options considered "traditional" in his or her social and economic context but also career options that appear "nontraditional" in the client's perception of the world. For example, for a client whose father and grandfather both worked as a heavy machine operator, the thought of going to college to pursue occupations such as attorney, teacher, or computer operator may seem strange; however, it should never be assumed that clients want to engage in the same occupations as their parents.

APPLICATION OF THE DEVELOPMENTAL THEORIES

Following is a treatment plan developed for a client, and then a demonstration of how a career counselor, using the developmental theories, would counsel with the client.

Goals

1. Help the client learn more about her life-span issues.
2. Help the client learn more about her life-space issues.

3. Help the client better understand the socioeconomic factors influencing career development.

Objectives

1. Assess the client's vocational maturity.
2. Assess the client's vocational identity.
3. Assess the client's occupational self-concept.
4. Examine the client's life structure.
5. Examine the client's role interactions.
6. Assist the client with life redesign.
7. Explore the occupational background of the client's family.

Interventions

1. Identify developmental tasks related to the client's stage in the life span.
2. Ask the client to complete her career rainbow.
3. Ask the client to do a career autobiography.
4. Have the client take the Adult Career Concerns Inventory.
5. Have the client take the Career Exploration Inventory and the Myers-Briggs Type Indicator.
6. Ask the client to do an occupational genogram.

Counseling Process

Ginzberg believed that the career counseling process consisted primarily of identifying the client's current career decision-making stage. Regardless of the client's chronological age, the career counselor uses an interview and a variety of assessment instruments to determine how far into the process each client is. The objective of career counseling, then, is a matter of moving the client through each of the remaining stages until a career decision is made. The career counselor is very supportive and acts in a variety of roles including coach, consultant, and teacher. The career counseling process is primarily one of helping the client gather information about himself and occupations, and then use rational decision-making skills.

Career counselors using the life-span approach focus on the process of choosing and adjusting to the outcomes of the client's choices. In order to do so, career counselors should diagnose the following distinct aspects of the client's life span.

Objective 1: Assess the Client's Vocational Maturity. Super (1990) saw vocational maturity as the extent to which an individual has successfully completed his or her developmental tasks. He saw developmental tasks as the accomplishments of career developmental steps compared with other people of the same age. Specific career behaviors and attitudes are required for people to achieve developmental tasks. These are developmental tasks that clients need to resolve in order for their career to develop naturally. When working with a client, attempt to identify the major developmental tasks that the person has not completed. Remember that these are correlated with the life-span portion of Super's career rainbow. The developmental tasks that Super (1980) identifies include:

> *Growth (4–14 Years):* Person becomes concerned about the future and about acquiring competent work habits and attitudes.
>
> *Crystallization (14–18 Years):* Person formulates a general vocational goal through awareness of resources, interests, abilities, and values. He or she begins planning for a preferred occupation.
>
> *Specification (18–21 Years):* Person moves from tentative occupational preferences toward a specific occupational preference.
>
> *Implementation (21–24 Years):* Person completes training in the area of vocational preference and begins employment.
>
> *Stabilization (25–35 Years):* Person confirms choice of a preferred career by actual work experience.
>
> *Consolidation (35+ Years):* Person becomes established in career through advancement, status, and seniority.

You can use these developmental tasks as a guide to determine exactly how vocationally mature your client is. The career counselor will question Kathy concerning the number of developmental tasks she has mastered.

COUNSELOR: How far along are you in making a career decision?

CLIENT: I have some ideas about the kinds of things I might like, and I know some jobs that I know I would never like to do. However, I just don't know what my true interests and abilities are. I've thought about a few things, but I need help matching my interests and abilities with the best job.

Kathy seems to be dealing with Super's crystallization developmental task. Your job as the career counselor is to help her to master the crystallization task and the other remaining developmental tasks. You can help your clients to explore their career maturity by using several assessment instruments. For example, Crites (1973) developed the first assessment instrument to measure vocational maturity. The Career Maturity Inventory (CMI) was designed for use primarily with adolescents in high school. Super, Thompson, Lindeman, Jordaan, and Meyers (1981) later developed the Career Development Inventory (CDI) to measure the major dimensions of career maturity in adolescents and young adults. The Adult Career Concerns

Inventory (ACCI; Super, Thompson, & Lindeman, 1988) was subsequently developed to assess the degree and focus of adult career concerns. The ACCI helps career counselors to identify the developmental tasks and life stages currently in need of attention and would be the instrument to use with Kathy.

Objective 2: Assess the Client's Vocational Identity. Vocational identity is the possession of a clear and stable picture of one's goals, interests, values, and talents. It is an objective view of oneself. Quantitative assessment instruments are used to identify the client's interests, values, and aptitudes. Although he did not develop a specific instrument for assessing interests, Super (1986) did develop the Values Scale to measure a client's intrinsic and extrinsic values. Liptak (1992b), with feedback from Super, developed the Career Exploration Inventory (CEI) to be the first life-span, life-space interest assessment instrument. The CEI is developmental in nature because it measures interests in the past, those in the present, and those anticipated in the future. It measures the life space by measuring interest in the roles of work, leisure, and learning.

The career counselor would administer a variety of assessment instruments to help the client obtain a more objective view of herself. The client can assist you in the selection of appropriate instruments.

> COUNSELOR: O.k., Kathy, now that you have taken several assessment instruments, let's look at the results. On the Career Exploration Inventory, your response pattern indicates interest in Social Activities, Plants and Animals, and Physical Performing.
>
> CLIENT: Yes, I do like working with people. I have always enjoyed helping others. I like gardening in my spare time. Working outdoors is fun and relaxing. The physical performing aspect is probably because I enjoy yoga and jogging.
>
> COUNSELOR: So gardening and working out are things you enjoy in your leisure time, but you would not like to do them as a job, and working with people is something you might like to do occupationally.
>
> CLIENT: Yeah, I guess so!
>
> COUNSELOR: Now let's look at the results of the values inventory and aptitude test you took.

The career counselor would systematically look at the results from all of Kathy's assessment instruments. You should rely on the client to be an active participant in this interpretation process. You should help the client to assess the results of the various instruments to form an initial idea of the types of occupations that may be a good match.

Objective 3: Assess the Client's Occupational Self-Concept. How clients see themselves is critical in making effective career choices. Occupational self-concept is the client's conceptions of herself. Super (1985) sees occupational self-concept as the client's subjective view of her life and the themes that permeate that life. He believed that the occupation to which the client is most attracted is the ideal self-concept. The greater the correlation between the client's choice of an occupation and the mental picture she has of an ideal occupation, the greater the client's career and life satisfaction. The career counselor's job is to help their clients develop an ideal self-concept by discovering outlets for their interests, values, aptitudes, and personality traits. On the other hand, if there is little correlation between the client's image and the work she is doing, the less career and life satisfaction she will possess. Several qualitative techniques for helping clients to identify their ideal self-concept have already been discussed.

The career counselor has Kathy do a career autobiography so he can help her understand more about herself by reflecting back to her his impressions of the major life themes that have influenced her career development.

> COUNSELOR: Kathy, based on interviews with you and after reading your career autobiography, I have identified several themes that appear evident throughout your career development. These themes seem to keep appearing as you are about to make important career decisions. You seem to feel extremely anxious about making important career decisions. I think you have a lot of irrational thoughts and self-defeating talk going on in your head. It's almost like you're afraid you will make the wrong decision so you don't make any decision at all. This fear and anxiety associated with making the perfect decision almost paralyzes you until you are not able to make any decisions. I think that a lot of this might be related to the stereotypes to which you were exposed as a child. Kathy, you also seem to have a low opinion of your own abilities (low self-esteem). You may often worry too much about what others think about you. Do these themes sound pretty accurate to you? (checking out the client to get her perspective about what has been said)
>
> CLIENT: Yes, I think that's a pretty accurate picture of me. I think that I am a perfectionist, and that's something I'm working on. I also worry about how I am perceived, and I do talk myself out of making some decisions. I don't think that I have low self-esteem though. (client verifies some of career counselor's impressions and disagrees with one of them)

The career counselor would work with Kathy to examine the content of the career themes that have been identified in their session. Much of the counseling would be centered around helping Kathy to find ways to lessen the impact of these themes on her career.

Objective 4: Examine the Client's Life Structure. Life structure indicates the social positions that clients play at the time they complete Super's career rainbow. The clients illustrate their pattern of core and peripheral roles in which they are currently engaged. The career counselor should help the client to explore the variety of roles and the amount of time she spends in each of the roles.

The career counselor working with Kathy asked her to develop her own career rainbow to identify problems related to her life space (see Figure 7.3). After looking at Kathy's rainbow, the career counselor noticed that she is engaging in the following roles: Mother, Student, Worker, Spouse, Child, Homemaker, and Leisurite.

> COUNSELOR: I see you have completed your career rainbow, Kathy. Let's talk about what you found out.
>
> CLIENT: O.k.
>
> COUNSELOR: Talk to me about the roles you have played over the years and the ones you are currently playing.
>
> CLIENT: Well . . . I guess I didn't realize how much I really do! How many ways I'm being pulled!

Figure 7.3   Career rainbow used by Kathy

Name _____

The Career Rainbow Summary Sheet for Ages 25–35

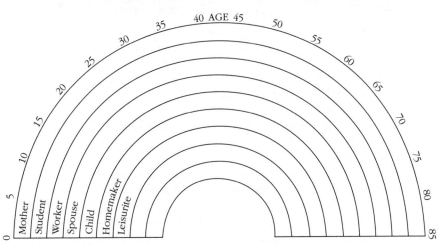

Assume that you are 25–35 years old, and that you have reached the "Getting Settled" life stage. You may then be spending some time and energy in several or most roles of the Career Rainbow. Make a check mark in front of each role that you would like to be playing at that age, and then briefly describe each of your roles as you hope it will be.

COUNSELOR: Tell me more about your rainbow.

CLIENT: Well, I'm a mother to Renee, a student at the college, I work a full-time job, a spouse to my husband, a child to my parents, I keep house, and I engage in leisure activities when I find time.

COUNSELOR: Wow, that's a lot! Where do you find the time to do all those things?

CLIENT: I don't know, I guess I had never thought about it.

COUNSELOR: Well, I'd like you to think about it now. I noticed that you said you were raising Renee, rather than *we* are raising her. Does Kerry help you?

CLIENT: He does a little . . . he's very tied down at work. He's a manager and is working ten-hour shifts. When he comes home, he is very tired!

COUNSELOR: So, you're primarily responsible for Renee and her needs?

CLIENT: Yes, I guess so.

COUNSELOR: What other roles are you engaged in currently?

CLIENT: Well, I am taking a course at the community college in Social Work, but it only meets once a week for a couple of hours. I am very involved in gardening around the house. I am a homemaker to Kerry. I am a child to my parents who live in Pittsburgh.

COUNSELOR: Your parents must be getting older. How often do you go to visit them?

CLIENT: We go about every two to three months and stay for several days if possible.

Objective 5: Examine the Client's Role Interactions. Role interactions include the interaction of multiple roles that enriches life or overburdens it. The career counselor should help clients to evaluate the effects of their life roles and the impact role interaction is having on their career and lives.

COUNSELOR: You seem stressed because you are stretched too thin. Do you think it's too many roles?

CLIENT: Maybe.

COUNSELOR: Are there any of your current roles that you could eliminate?

CLIENT: Well, I am married to Kerry, a very nice guy. We have been married for eleven years now. Our marriage is great. I'm raising my daughter, Renee, who's 10. That's a lot of work, but I love it. My job is o.k. I am taking a course at the college that I could give up. I enjoy doing yardwork. I guess the housework is what is getting me down. I think, though, that if I could get a job that I liked better, some of these other roles might not be so stressful.

COUNSELOR: O.k., the course does take time during your week. I'm sure you must read, go to the library, and write papers. However,

I feel this exposure to social work is important to your career development. You said you enjoy the class and may consider work with troubled kids as a career option.

CLIENT: That's true.

COUNSELOR: I agree that you need to explore some additional career options. But the household also seems to be where you need some assistance.

Objective 6: Assist the Client with Life Redesign. Life redesign is helping clients to recognize that they have some control over the roles they play and the amount of time they spend engaged in each role. Career counselors should help clients deal with the feelings of traumatic situations and assist them in building a new life plan.

COUNSELOR: You are a very busy person. How could we rework some of the roles you are currently engaged in so that you will feel less stress?

CLIENT: I don't know. I don't think I could give anything up.

COUNSELOR: What if you could get Kerry to help you more with the household chores? Could he help you clean or cook, or help take care of your child?

CLIENT: I think I could talk with him about it. Maybe he doesn't know how busy I am!

COUNSELOR: Good. How about your job? How much do you like it?

CLIENT: I tolerate it. It isn't what I want to do for the rest of my life.

COUNSELOR: What is? A higher paying job . . . one with more prestige . . . one where you are making a difference?

CLIENT: Yes.

COUNSELOR: Have you thought about quitting your job and going back to school . . . or working part-time and going back to school?

CLIENT: That's a possibility I really had not thought about.

The Salience Inventory (SI; Super & Nevill, 1985) measures the relative importance of five major life roles including student, worker, homemaker, leisurite, and citizen. The SI was designed to measure an individual's actual and anticipated participation in and commitment to a variety of life roles. The SI can be used with adolescents and adults to measure career commitment and occupational involvement, as well as to assist the client in the examination of her involvement in study, home and family, leisure activities, and community service.

Objective 7: Explore the Occupational Background of the Client's Family. Genograms are an excellent tool for career counselors to use to gather information about the careers of the client's significant others. The technique is used primarily by family therapists (e.g., Bowen, 1980), but it has been described for use in career counseling (Gysbers & Moore, 1987; Okiishi, 1987). Brown and Brooks (1991) recommend the use of genograms and describe them as a "graphic representation of the careers of the client's biological and step-grandparents, parents, aunts and uncles, and siblings" (p. 126). Okiishi (1987) notes that the family of origin is the crucial variable in the development of a person's attitudes about himself; it also influences the way a person sees himself fitting into the world, including various occupations. Therefore, career counselors can use career genograms to help clients explore how the occupations of significant others affect our views of self and the world-of-work.

> COUNSELOR: O.k., Kathy, now I want you to tell me about your family history. To help you with this, I'm going to ask you to do a career genogram for me.
> CLIENT: What's a career genogram?
> COUNSELOR: It's a diagram of the careers of your parents, grandparents, siblings, and other significant others.
> CLIENT: My family's pretty average!
> COUNSELOR: Let's just do one and see what we come up with . . . o.k.?
> CLIENT: O.k.

(See Kathy's genogram in Figure 7.4.)

Figure 7.4   Kathy's genogram
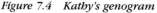

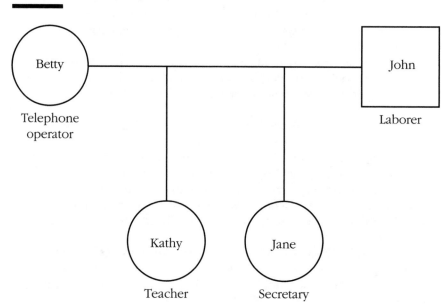

COUNSELOR: Please describe now, Kathy, what you have drawn.

CLIENT: My mother and father are still living in the Pittsburgh area. My mother is retired from Bell Telephone where she was a telephone operator, and my father worked as a laborer for Columbia Gas Company. My older sister and her husband are raising two sons, George and Jackson.

COUNSELOR: What does your sister do for a living?

CLIENT: She is a secretary and receptionist for a small medical practice.

COUNSELOR: How satisfied were your parents in their occupations?

CLIENT: They were very satisfied. They loved their jobs, or at least that's what I saw and what they said.

COUNSELOR: Did they go to college?

CLIENT: No, neither of them had the opportunity to do so, but they encouraged us very much to do so.

COUNSELOR: But your sister chose not to go?

CLIENT: Correct . . . she wanted to go to secretarial school . . . I think. She seems to really like what she's doing.

The career counselor also wants to explore the relationship between the number of years of schooling Kathy has completed and the level of education of her parents. In addition, he will explore the implicit status level of her parents.

COUNSELOR: You said your parents both liked their jobs, right?

CLIENT: Yes.

COUNSELOR: They both were employed in service positions?

CLIENT: Yes, as a telephone operator, my mother was able to talk with and help people all day. She likes that—she is a very social person. My father was not as social, but he liked being able to provide a service to other people.

COUNSELOR: You told me earlier that your parents encouraged you and your sister to go to college. So even though they had never gone, they wanted you to. Tell me more about this.

Notice that the career counselor explores not only the socioeconomic status of her parents' jobs but also the amount of encouragement that Kathy received from her parents to go to college. This gives the career counselor some sense of the relative importance that education played in Kathy's household as she was growing up.

CHAPTER 8

CONCEPTUALIZING COGNITIVE THEORIES

It is important to examine how learning has affected your clients' perceptions of themselves and of the world. Learning and the processing of information are crucial in a person's career development. Learning affects people's attitudes as well as behaviors.

This chapter discusses the second premise of an eclectic approach discussed in Chapter 1: *People continually acquire and process accurate, as well as inaccurate, career information about themselves and the world. This information is gained through a variety of life experiences and often forces people to operate under inaccurate suppositions about themselves and the world-of-work.* This chapter builds upon this premise by showing career counselors how to examine the client's belief system, monitor the client's cognitive information processing, and determine the client's self-efficacy beliefs.

KRUMBOLTZ'S SOCIAL LEARNING THEORY OF CAREER DECISION MAKING

Krumboltz (1979) was primarily interested in developing a practical theory that career counselors could use in practice to intervene constructively and help clients solve their career-related problems. His social learning theory of career decision making (SLTCDM) is derived from the general social learning theory of behavior (Bandura, 1977).

Social learning theory postulates that people develop personalities and behavioral repertoires through their unique learning experiences. People, at the same time, attempt to control their environments to suit their own unique needs. Krumboltz (1979) believes that interests develop as a consequence of learning. He also believes that learning, not interests or abilities, is what leads people to certain occupations. Furthermore, changes in learning produce changes in interests and occupational preferences. The social learning theory of career decision making was designed to help determine why people enter certain occupations, why people change occupations, and why people prefer various occupations at different points in their lives.

Krumboltz (1979) believes that the following types of factors influence the career decision-making process for people:

1. *Genetic Endowment and Special Abilities:* These are inherited qualities that make each person unique. These qualities influence the client's choice of occupational and educational activities and include such things as ethnicity, gender, physique, and special abilities.

2. *Environmental Conditions and Events:* These factors are outside of the client's control. Included in this category are such things as the number of job opportunities available for the client in the area in which he or she is seeking a job, labor laws and union rules, catastrophic events such as floods and earthquakes, government policies, the number and nature of various training opportunities, technological developments, and job requirements for prospective employers.

3. *Learning Experiences:* A person encounters different types of learning experiences throughout a lifetime. *Instrumental* learning experiences are those in which the client is positively reinforced or negatively reinforced for some behavior. People repeat those behaviors for which they receive positive reinforcement and avoid those behaviors for which they receive no reinforcement or negative reinforcement. For example, a client who has been praised for teaching a lesson to his classmates may decide that teaching is an appropriate career choice. *Associative* learning experiences are those in which the client indirectly or through observation of the behavior or response of others (vicarious learning) exhibits new behaviors and skills. For example, a client may decide not to go to law school because she hears her father say that "all lawyers are crooked."

As a result of the complex interaction among these influencing factors, people develop beliefs about themselves and the world-of-work. These beliefs, in turn, then influence people's ability to learn new skills and thus affect both behaviors and aspirations. These beliefs, which can be grouped into four categories, need to be examined by the career counselor.

1. *Self-Observation Generalizations:* In career counseling, you should be most concerned about how people view themselves and their ability to perform tasks required of certain occupations. In essence, people make assessments by comparing their performance to their own set of standards or standards established by significant others.

Similarly, as a result of instrumental and associative learning experiences, people tend to generalize about activities they like or do not like. Clients often have generalizations based on unrealistic or inaccurate information.

2. *World-View Generalizations:* People also make generalizations about the nature of various occupations and make predictions about how successful they can be in the occupational environment.

3. *Task Approach Skills:* This category refers to the special career-related skills and behaviors that must be possessed by clients in order for them to make good career decisions and solve career problems. These skills include work habits, values, and decision-making skills.

4. *Actions:* People eventually enter the world-of-work by entering into an occupation or a training program.

Krumboltz's theory focuses on occupational choice and entry into an occupation or a training program for an occupation. Propositions for the theory state:

1. An individual is more likely to enter an occupation if he or she (a) has been positively reinforced for activities related to that occupation, (b) has seen a valued model be positively reinforced for activities related to that occupation, (c) has been positively reinforced by a valued person who advocates that he or she engage in that occupation, or (d) has been exposed to positive words or images relating to that occupation.

2. A person is less likely to engage in an occupation or its related training and activities if he or she (a) has been punished or not reinforced for engaging in related activities, (b) has observed a valued model being punished or not reinforced for those activities, or (c) has been reinforced by a valued model who expresses negative words or images related to the occupation.

3. An individual is more likely to learn appropriate career decision-making skills if he or she (a) has been reinforced for those activities, (b) has observed a model be reinforced for those activities, and (c) has access to people and other resources with the necessary information.

4. An individual is less likely to learn appropriate career decision-making skills if he or she (a) has been punished or not reinforced for those behaviors, (b) has observed a model be punished or not reinforced for those behaviors, or (c) has little or no access to people and other resources with the necessary information.

5. An individual is more likely to enter an occupation if that individual (a) has recently expressed a preference for that occupation, (b) has been exposed to learning and employment opportunities in

that field, and (c) has learned skills that match the requirements of the occupation.

6. An individual is less likely to enter an occupation if the individual (a) finds the cost of preparation to be greater than the eventual return or (b) is denied access to the minimum resources necessary for entering the occupation.

SOCIAL-COGNITIVE CAREER THEORY

Betz and Hackett (1981) and Hackett (1985) wrote about women's self-efficacy beliefs concerning their mathematical ability. These self-efficacy beliefs, these theorists believe, had an influence on women's participation in math-related occupations, even for those women who did not demonstrate a deficiency in math skills. Hackett and Betz (1981) describe a self-efficacy approach to the career development of women. In their theory, the social-cognitive career theory (SCCT; Lent, Brown, & Hackett, 1994), the focus is on the learning processes that lead to beliefs and how these beliefs impact the career decision-making process and lead to career behaviors.

The social-cognitive career theory is based on Bandura's (1969) cognitive social learning theory, which proposes that an individual has efficacy expectations about a behavior and its probable consequence, thus influencing how much effort she will exert on the behavior. Following are the important elements in the SCCT:

Self-Efficacy: "People's beliefs about their capability to organize and execute courses of action required to attain designated types of performances" (Bandura, 1986, p. 391). Self-efficacy is seen as a dynamic set of beliefs, acquired through learning and specific to particular performance domains, that answers the question "Can I do this?" Self-efficacy is raised through success experiences and lowered through failure experiences.

Outcome Expectations: Personal beliefs about the outcomes of performing particular behaviors (Bandura, 1986). Outcome expectations answer the question "If I do this, what will happen?" These beliefs are also acquired through a variety of learning experiences.

Personal Goals: Determination to engage in a particular activity or to have an effect on future outcomes (Bandura, 1986). Clients control their future by using goals to organize and guide their future behaviors.

These three factors interact and affect the client's career decision making. For example, self-efficacy affects a client's beliefs about engaging in certain occupations; thus, a client may not set a goal to gather information about certain occupations. The career choice process (see Figure 8.1) incorporates interest development, the development of goals and making choices, taking action, and subsequent successes and failure.

In this model, the client brings with him certain personal and contextual variables that affect the career development process. Personal variables include such factors as gender, race/ethnicity, physical health and disabilities, and genetic endowment. Contextual variables include such factors as socioeconomic status, family dynamics, living situation, relationship status, and current support system. These factors thus expose the client to a variety of work and leisure activities that are relevant in the career development process. While pursuing these activities, the client receives negative or positive reinforcement. The reinforcement received in these activities determines the client's self-efficacy and outcome expectations. Self-efficacy and outcome expectations determine career-related interests; interests then influence the client's goals; goals stimulate an action plan; and the behavior of this action plan leads to performance experiences. These performance experiences either verify the client's self-efficacy, outcome expectations, and career choice, or they do not—in which case the process begins anew at the learning experiences phase.

COGNITIVE INFORMATION-PROCESSING APPROACH

The cognitive information-processing approach (CIP; Peterson, Sampson, & Reardon, 1991) is primarily concerned with thought and memory processes involved in solving career problems and making career decisions. The CIP model draws on work of Donald Michenbaum and stresses that career problem-solving is a cognitive process based on the following assumptions:

1. Career problem solving and decision making involve affective as well as cognitive processes. Emotions are also an integral component of career decision making. Such emotions as anxiety, depression, confusion, and fright may be present during any of the career problem-solving phases.
2. The career decision-making process is a problem-solving activity. Although complex and somewhat ambiguous, clients can learn to solve career problems. The career counselor's job is to identify the client's needs and problems, then acquire the knowledge and develop the skills to meet those particular needs.
3. The capability for career problem solving depends on the availability of cognitive operations as well as knowledge. These cognitive operations include such functions as storing occupational

Figure 8.1   Career choice process

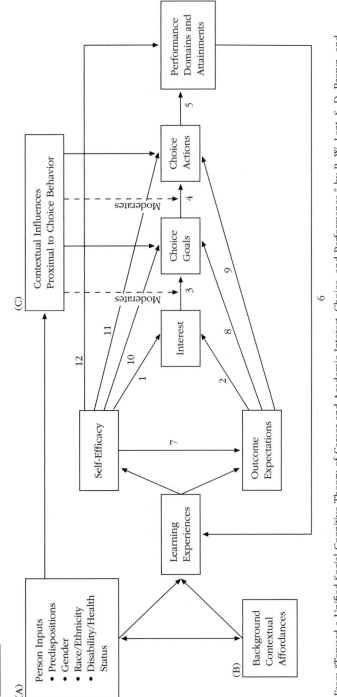

From "Toward a Unified Social Cognitive Theory of Career and Academic Interest, Choice, and Performance," by R. W. Lent, S. D. Brown, and G. Hackett, *Journal of Vocational Behavior*, 1993, vol. 45, pp. 79–122. Copyright © 1993, Academic Press, Inc. Reprinted by permission.

knowledge in long-term memory, transforming information into meaningful forms, and solving and evaluating career decisions.

4. Career problem solving is a high-memory-load task. Self-knowledge and occupational knowledge are both complex domains that must be integrated simultaneously for constructive career decision making.

5. Clients are motivated through the integration of self-knowledge and occupational knowledge to make satisfying career decisions.

6. Career development involves continual growth and change in knowledge structures. As clients acquire self-knowledge and occupational knowledge, networks of memory structures develop, and this knowledge is integrated over the client's life span.

7. Career identity depends on self-knowledge. The clarity and stability of the information contained in the self-knowledge domain constitute the client's career identity.

8. Career maturity depends on the client's ability to solve career problems. The ability of the client to successfully integrate self-knowledge and occupational knowledge defines the client's career maturity.

9. The development of career problem-solving and decision-making skills is accomplished through the enhancement of information-processing capabilities. Career counselors must provide the appropriate conditions for clients to acquire self-knowledge and occupational information, develop career problem-solving skills, and develop a career action plan.

10. The ultimate aim of career counseling is to enhance the client's capabilities as a career problem solver and decision maker.

To become effective career problem solvers and decision makers, clients must fully develop their information-processing capabilities. These information-processing capabilities may be seen as skills that are hierarchically arranged from basic (self-knowledge and occupational knowledge) to sophisticated (metacognitions). Peterson, Sampson, and Reardon (1991) developed a pyramid of information-processing domains of the decision-making process (see Figure 8.2).

Following is a description of the four information-processing skills:

1. *Knowing about self (self-knowledge):* Gathering information about the client through the use of qualitative exercises and quantitative assessment instruments

2. *Knowing about career options (occupational knowledge):* Descriptions of work environments gained through computer-assisted guidance systems, shadowing workers, talking with

Figure 8.2   Pyramid of information-processing domains

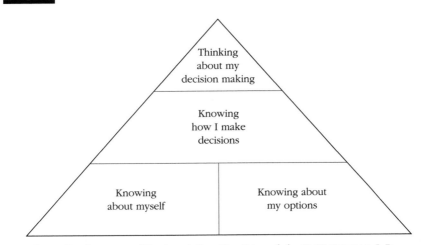

From *Career Development and Services: A Cognitive Approach,* by G. W. Peterson, J. P. Sampson, and R. C. Reardon. Copyright © 1991, Brooks/Cole.

employees in the occupation of interest to the client, and using audiovisual materials and various career information resources

3. *Knowing how I make career decisions (CASVE):* Information from the self-knowledge and occupational knowledge domains is processed to make appropriate decisions, and a strategy for implementation of the decisions is developed (This process is described in more detail in Figure 8.3.)

4. *Thinking about my decision making (metacognitions):* Examining the client's dysfunctional, irrational thought patterns

Peterson, Sampson, and Reardon (1991), in their book *Career Development and Services: A Cognitive Approach,* describe five stages of the career decision-making process. They title this the CASVE stage, or the decision-making skills domain, of the model and believe it is comprised of the stages shown in Figure 8.3.

APPLICATION OF THE COGNITIVE THEORIES

Following is a treatment plan developed for a client, and then a demonstration of how a career counselor, using the cognitive theories, would counsel with the client.

Figure 8.3   *The five stages of the CASVE cycle of information-processing skills used*
▬▬▬▬▬   *in career decision making*

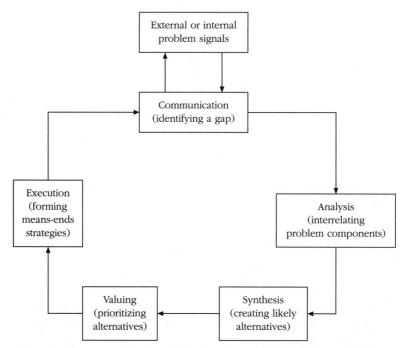

From *Career Development and Services: A Cognitive Approach,* by G. W. Peterson, J. P. Sampson, and R. C. Reardon. Copyright © 1991, Brooks/Cole Publishing Company, Pacific Grove, CA 93950, a division of International Thomson Publishing Inc.

Goals

1. Gather realistic occupational information.
2. Correct irrational and dysfunctional beliefs.
3. Explore the client's approach to information processing.

Objectives

1. Identify patterns of irrational thinking.
2. Identify insufficient task approach skills.
3. Examine the client's self-efficacy beliefs.
4. Help clients process information about occupations of interest.

Interventions

1. Administer the Career Beliefs Inventory.
2. Teach the client task approach skills.

3. Help the client identify sources of occupational information.
4. Monitor the client's self-talk.
5. Encourage client to complete the SIGI+.

Counseling Process

Objective 1: Identify Patterns of Irrational Thinking. Krumboltz (1994) views the career development process as an intercorrelated sequence of learning experiences. He believes that the job of the career counselor is to facilitate learning. Most people are exposed to a limited variety of learning experiences. Career counselors must attempt to design new learning experiences for their clients. Clients who are undecided about which occupations to enter suffer from a deficit in information, not problems with development. Career counseling, therefore, is the process of helping clients identify their learning experiences and motivating them to initiate career-related exploratory activities.

Krumboltz believes that clients come to career counseling with a variety of irrational beliefs about themselves and the world-of-work. The career counselor should be alert to these irrational beliefs and help clients to examine all available evidence about their beliefs. This is best accomplished by simply asking for evidence of a belief. This evidence is best examined by asking clients to give you specific examples to either support or disprove the belief. The career counselor should also monitor clients' self-talk. In this technique, the career counselor helps the client listen to the negative talk that is going on in her head when making career decisions. The client can be taught to use a journal to record her self-talk and replace negative statements with more positive statements.

Zunker (1994), in citing Krumboltz (1983), suggests that career counselors need to be alert to the following types of problems exhibited by their clients: persons may fail to recognize that a remediable problem exists (individuals assume that most problems are a normal part of life and cannot be altered); persons may fail to exert the effort needed to make a decision or solve a problem (individuals exert little effort to explore alternatives and often take the familiar way out); persons may eliminate a potentially satisfying alternative for an inappropriate reason (individuals overgeneralize from false assumptions and overlook potentially worthwhile alternatives); persons may choose poor alternatives for inappropriate reasons (individuals may be unable to realistically evaluate potential careers because of false beliefs and unrealistic expectations); and persons may suffer anguish and anxiety over perceived inability to achieve goals (individual goals may be unrealistic or in conflict with other goals).

COUNSELOR: Let's talk a little bit about the course you are taking in Social Work. How do you like it?

CLIENT: I love the class, but it's hard zgoing to back school after being out so long.

COUNSELOR: Would you enjoy working at that type of an occupation?

CLIENT: I would . . . I think. But I'd never be good at that type of work. (self-observation generalization)

COUNSELOR: What makes you say that? (counselor asks for evidence of this belief)

CLIENT: I could never do that for a living. I can teach, but I could never help people solve their problems!

COUNSELOR: How do you know that? I thought you said that you enjoyed the mentoring aspect of teaching? (counselor asks for evidence of this belief)

CLIENT: I guess I just never thought about anything but teaching as an occupation. But I would never be able to go to graduate school. (self-observation generalization)

COUNSELOR: How do you know that you could not do master's-level work? (counselor asks for evidence of this belief) What were your grades in high school and college?

CLIENT: I graduated with a 3.5 GPA in both.

COUNSELOR: So then you could easily do the work. You just sound a little scared about the thought of going to graduate school.

CLIENT: I am a little scared. I don't know if I could keep up the pace. I've got my daughter at home, and it's been a long time since I've been in school. All the other students would be much younger and probably much smarter than me. (world-view generalization) I'm worried that I might fail!

COUNSELOR: We need to talk about some of your irrational thoughts about yourself and your abilities. (At this point, the career counselor would begin to examine how her irrational thinking keeps her from taking risks. By helping her to reframe her situation and examine the way she catastrophizes about the possibility of failing, the counselor will help her see the opportunity of graduate school in a much different light.)

COUNSELOR: Maybe you ought to think about a career helping people other than teaching.

CLIENT: But there aren't many jobs for social workers. (world-view generalization) And the jobs that are available don't pay that much money. (world-view generalization)

COUNSELOR: How do you know? Have you talked with any people working in that particular occupational field? Do you know anyone doing this kind of work? Have you ever read about the salary structure for social workers? Did you know that there are many more occupations than social workers that help people including counselors, geriatric workers, psychiatric technicians, and probation officers to name a few?

CLIENT: No . . . I guess my reaction is my stereotype of those types of occupations . . . not based on accurate information.

COUNSELOR: Let's take a look at some occupational information related to some of these occupational fields. (At this point, the career counselor would use a variety of types of career information resources to help the client gather reliable information about the world-of-work.)

The Career Beliefs Inventory (CBI) was developed by Krumboltz (1991) to help clients and counselors in identifying troublesome beliefs that may be blocking the client's career development. The CBI contains twenty-five scales that are organized into five major groups. These five groups include My Current Situation, What Seems Necessary for My Happiness, Factors That Influence My Decisions, Changes I Am Willing to Make, and Effort I Am Willing to Initiate. Scores on the scales indicate whether a particular belief is blocking or facilitating the client's progress.

Objective 2: Identify Insufficient Task Approach Skills. Krumboltz (1983) feels that clients need to be taught the process for effective decision making and problem solving. He suggests the following method in which the career counselor helps the client to:

1. recognize and understand that an important career decision must be made;
2. realistically define the task at hand;
3. examine self-observations and world-view generalizations;
4. generate alternatives;
5. gather accurate information about the various alternatives; and
6. eliminate alternatives that are inappropriate for the career decision.

Objective 3: Examine the Client's Self-Efficacy Beliefs. Career counselors often learn that how a client sees himself or sees a situation dictates how he feels about that situation. By reframing the situation, the career counselor can bring the client closer to reality.

COUNSELOR: Now that you have gathered some basic occupational information, tell me a little bit about some of the occupations that you choose to examine closer and some that you choose not to explore. Let's start first with those that you have no interest in. (This will allow the career counselor to explore occupations in which she feels high self-efficacy and occupations she would not choose due to low self-efficacy beliefs.)

CLIENT: Well, I think I would not like scientific occupations like botanist or biologist or occupations working with tools and machines.

COUNSELOR: O.k., tell me now about some of the occupations that you are interested in gathering occupational information about.

CLIENT: I seem to like the jobs in which I would work with people, like counselors, college professors, social workers. I also like artistic things like maybe teaching art.

COUNSELOR: Let's talk about some of the jobs you have had in the past. How effectively did you see yourself using certain skills in your previous jobs?

The career counselor attempts to determine Kathy's self-appraisal about certain skills she used in previous occupations. You should thoroughly explore how capable your clients see themselves using the skills required in occupations currently held or those held in the past.

COUNSELOR: How supportive is your family in this process of your looking for a job? (looking at one of the main contextual variables)

CLIENT: Well, my husband is very supportive. He wants me to do well . . . to succeed.

COUNSELOR: O.k. Now let's develop an array of occupational possibilities that correspond with your aptitudes, values, and personality. Based on the information you have available, what would those occupations be?

CLIENT: Well, it looks like college teaching, child care, art instructor, counselor, art therapist, and social worker may be good matches.

COUNSELOR: How do you see yourself in each of these occupations? (helping the client to re-evaluate her self-efficacy beliefs about each occupation)

Objective 4: Help Clients Process Information About Occupations of Interest. First, help clients learn about themselves. Clients often have unrealistic beliefs about their abilities, interests, values, and personality characteristics. The career counselor can help clients dispute these beliefs by helping them identify information about themselves. This self-exploration can be done with standardized assessment instruments or by just having the client talk and think about himself.

Second, help clients learn about the world-of-work. Clients often have unrealistic beliefs about the work world. These beliefs come in the form of misinformation concerning job specifications such as a job's salary, working conditions, employment outlook, and educational or training requirements. The career counselor can help clients dispute these beliefs by helping them gather information about occupations. This occupational exploration can be done through the use of print media such as the DOT and GOE, videos about certain occupations, computer-assisted career counseling programs such as SIGI Plus and Discover, occupational simulations, and shadowing workers.

The career counselor now needs to help Kathy gather and process information about each of these occupations. To get realistic outcome expectations, the client should be directed to various sources of occupational information. Then she will need help in exploring barriers in getting the job she would like, assessing the match between the job and the reinforcers of that job, preparing for additional study if needed, and developing career coping strategies (goal-setting strategies).

> COUNSELOR: I think at this point we need to define the problem you are having. (attempting to determine the gap that exists between where Kathy is and where she would like to be)
>
> CLIENT: I now have some ideas about what occupation I would like to start working in. I have learned a lot about myself and the factors that have influenced my career so far. What I think I need now is to gather some information about the occupations of interest to me.
>
> COUNSELOR: I agree. Why do you think that is? (asking Kathy to reflect and analyze why this problem exists)
>
> CLIENT: I just have been pretty sheltered and I have not had a chance to do a lot of career exploration.
>
> COUNSELOR: How do you think we can help you to obtain more occupational information?
>
> CLIENT: I could talk with people working in those occupations or maybe shadow one of them. I could also read some books or maybe look for information on the Internet.
>
> COUNSELOR: Yes, Kathy, very good! You maybe could also work with SIGI Plus, watch some videos on different occupations, or look at some career reference books. Could you prioritize the courses of action that suit you the best?
>
> CLIENT: Yes, I think I can access information from the Internet most easily. Then I think I would like to look at some print material, maybe reference books. It is going to be difficult for me to talk with or shadow employees, but I may be able to in about a week or so. Working on the SIGI Plus computer does not sound very interesting to me, but I could give it a try.
>
> COUNSELOR: O.k., let's develop a plan for you to visit the career resource center to start your search for occupational information.

At this point, the career counselor would help Kathy to develop a concrete action plan for implementing her strategies for enhancing her problem-solving and decision-making skills. The career counselor would also explore how her thinking has influenced her action plan. An individual learning plan can be developed to help your clients to be as intentional as possible.

 CHAPTER 9

CONCEPTUALIZING MATCHING THEORIES

Career counseling theories that match the individual with appropriate occupations have been used since the time of Frank Parsons (1909) in the early 1900s. These types of theories are still being used in many career counseling settings. This chapter examines the third premise of the comprehensive approach to career counseling discussed in Chapter 1: *Career choice ultimately involves a matching of the characteristics of the individual with those of the work environment.* This chapter builds upon this premise by showing career counselors how to examine the client's personality, examine the client's early childhood experiences, and match the client's traits with factors of an occupation.

HOLLAND'S PERSONALITY THEORY

Holland's (1973) theory classifies people and work environments into six personality types. He believes that individuals search for work environments that allow them to express their personality. In using his theory, career counselors concentrate on matching people and congruent occupations in an attempt to attain occupational satisfaction. Career counseling, therefore, involves resolving incongruence by seeking a new and congruent environment or by changing personal behavior and perceptions.

In an attempt to develop an elegant and symmetrical theory, Holland (1992) identified a number of basic principles including:

- The choice of a vocation is an expression of personality.
- Interest inventories are personality inventories.
- Vocational stereotypes have reliable and important psychological and sociological meanings.
- The members of a vocation have similar personalities and similar histories of personal development.

- Because people in a vocational group have similar personalities, they will respond to many situations and problems in similar ways, and they will create characteristic interpersonal environments.
- Vocational satisfaction, stability, and achievement depend on the congruence between one's personality and the environment in which one works (pp. 7–11).

Based on these assumptions about human nature, Holland (1992) provided the following overview of his model.

Types of People and Work Environments

In our culture, most persons and work environments can be categorized as one of the six types that follow.

Realistic. This person values concrete and physical tasks, perceives self as having mechanical skills and lacking social skills, and has a preference for activities that include the explicit, ordered, or systematic manipulation of tools, objects, machines, and animals. This work setting involves concrete, physical tasks requiring mechanical skills, persistence, and physical movement. Careers include machine operator, aircraft mechanic, truck driver, service station worker, draftsperson, barber, and bricklayer.

Investigative. This person wants to solve intellectual, scientific, and mathematical problems; sees self as scholarly, analytic, critical, curious, introspective, and methodical; and has a preference for activities that include the observational, symbolic, systematic, and creative investigation of physical, biological, and cultural phenomena. This work setting involves such things as a research laboratory, diagnostic medical case conference, or work group of scientists or medical researchers. Careers include marine biologist, computer programmer, clinical psychologist, architect, dentist, mathematician, and physical scientist.

Artistic. This person prefers unsystematic tasks or artistic projects in the form of painting, writing, or drama; perceives self as imaginative, expressive, original, and independent; and has a preference for ambiguous, free, unsystematized activities that include the manipulation of physical, verbal, or human materials to create art forms or products. This work setting involves such things as a theater, concert hall, library, or radio or television studio. Careers include painter, sculptor, actor or actress, designer, musician, music teacher, symphony conductor, author, editor, reviewer, and radio or television announcer.

Social. This person prefers educational, religious, and helping careers; enjoys such activities as social involvement, church, music, reading, and dramatics; perceives self as having understanding, liking to help others, and having teaching ability; and has a preference for activities that include the manipulation of others to inform, train, develop, cure, or enlighten. A social person values social or ethical activities and is cooperative, friendly, helpful, insightful, persuasive, responsible, and sociable. This work setting includes such things as a college classroom, psychiatrist's office, religious meeting, mental health institution, or community and recreational center. Careers include counselor, nurse, teacher, social worker, judge, missionary, minister, and sociologist.

Enterprising. This person values political and economic achievements, supervision, and leadership; enjoys activities that satisfy personal need for control, verbal expression, recognition, and power; perceives self as extroverted, sociable, happy, assertive, popular, self-confident, and as having leadership and persuasive abilities; and has a preference for activities that include the manipulation of others to attain organizational goals or economic gain. This work setting includes such things as a courtroom, political rally, new car show room, real estate firm, and an advertising company. Careers include politician, realtor, attorney, professional orator, salesperson, and manager.

Conventional. This person prefers orderly, systematic, concrete tasks involving verbal and mathematical data; sees self as orderly, conformist, and having clerical and numerical skills; and has a preference for activities that include the explicit, ordered, systematic manipulation of data, such as keeping records, filing materials, reproducing materials, organizing written and numerical data according to a prescribed plan, and operating business machines and data processing machines to attain organizational or economic goals. This work setting involves such things as financial institution (bank), accounting firm, post office, file room, business office, and Internal Revenue office. Careers include accountant, banker, tax expert, timekeeper, financial counselor, secretary, computer operator, and receptionist.

Matching People to Work Environments

Given these six types of personality and work environments, people search for environments that will let them exercise their skills and abilities, express their attitudes and values, and take on agreeable roles and problems.

Holland has developed several assessment instruments to measure a client's personality type. The Self-Directed Search (SDS; Holland, 1979) is a career guidance tool specifically designed to determine a person's resemblance to the six personality types and then relate them to specific occupations. The SDS uses activities, competencies, occupations, and self-ratings to establish a three-letter code comprised of the first letters of the person's three most prominent personality types. For example, a person who is primarily Social, then Artistic, and then Realistic would get a code of SAR. Clients then can look in the Occupations Finder to identify congruent occupations.

The Vocational Preference Inventory (VPI; Holland, 1977) is a brief assessment instrument that measures a person's interests. The VPI consists of 160 occupational titles that are grouped into scales taken from Holland's classification of six categories.

My Vocational Situation (MVS; Holland, 1980) measures a variety of problems that might be interfering with your client's career development. The MVS provides information about your client's vocational identity, lack of career information, and personal or environmental barriers to career development.

Interaction of People and Work Environments

Behavior is determined by an interaction between personality and environment. Holland believes that an individual with a realistic personality will function best in an environment in which he can work with tools, objects, animals, or technical equipment in mechanical activities. On the other hand, an individual with a social personality will function best in an environment in which he can work to help others, engage in social interaction, pursue educational activities, and do work that is community-service oriented. Everyone has a combination of different orientations with one orientation being dominant. For example, a person can be primarily a conventional personality type but also have some personality traits of realistic and artistic people; in ranking the traits from highest to lowest, this person's pattern of personality orientation might be conventional, realistic, and artistic.

ROE'S MODEL OF PERSONALITY

Roe's (1956) theory attempts to predict occupational choice based on the type of childhood relationships that clients have had with their parents. Roe states that experiences of childhood are related to career behavior and are the most important determinant of the occupation that is chosen. In essence, early childhood environments predispose children to enter into certain occupations. Roe believes that vocational choice helps satisfy a need and that people develop a certain lifestyle to meet their needs. Her ideas are based on Maslow's (1968) hierarchy of needs because that is the most direct method for relating the relevance of occupations to the satisfaction of basic needs.

Roe and Siegelman (1964) have stated the following propositions:

1. Genetic inheritance sets limits to the potential development of all characteristics, but the specificity of the genetic control and the extent and nature of the limitation are different for different characteristics.
2. The degrees and avenues of development of inherited characteristics are affected not only by experience unique to the individual but also by all aspects of the general cultural background and the socioeconomic position of the family.

3. The pattern of development of interests, attitudes, and other personality variables is first determined by the patterning of early satisfactions and frustrations (p. 5).

Roe's thoughts about career counseling and the influence of the parent
style of the client are interesting. The theory attempts to explain the influence
of early childhood experiences on your clients. Roe (1956) hypothesized that
there existed three categories of parental behavior with children. These categories and their subcategories are discussed in the following text.

Emotional Concentration on the Child

Protective parents give the child's interests first priority. They indulge
the child, give her special privileges, and are extremely affectionate. They are
careful who the child spends time with and even protect her from other children. They protect her from situations in which she may be disappointed or
injured. They intrude in the child's affairs and expect to know all the child is
thinking and feeling. They reward feelings of dependency in her.

Demanding parents set very high standards for the child. They demand
unquestioning obedience to them and impose strict regulations. They make
no exceptions to their demands. They expect the child to be busy at all times
and tend to be very punitive. Friendships of the child must meet their
approval. They care very little about what the child is thinking or feeling
because they tell her what to think and feel.

Avoidance of the Child

Rejecting parents either reject the childishness of the child or reject her
altogether. They appear cold and hostile. They may derogate her, make fun
of her, and have little empathy for her problems and inadequacies. They frequently leave her alone and may not permit other children in the house. They
do not regard the child's point of view. Regulations are established to protect
them from the child's intrusions, rather than for her sake.

Neglecting parents pay very little attention to the child. They give her a
minimum amount of care and little if any affection. They forget any promis-
es that have been made to the child. They tend to be cold, but not deroga-
tory or hostile. They leave her alone, but they do not go out of their way to
avoid her.

Acceptance of the Child

Casual parents pay some attention to the child and are mildly affectionate. They are responsive to her when they are not busy with anything

else. They spend little time thinking about the child or making plans with the child, but rather take her as part of their current situation. They do not worry much about her, and they make little effort to train her. They are easygoing, have very few rules for the child, and do not make much effort to enforce the rules they do have.

Loving parents give the child warm and loving attention. They help her with projects that are important to her. They are caring, but do not intrude on the child's privacy. They will reason with the child rather than punish her. They praise the child when appropriate. They develop a trusting relationship so that the child feels able to confide in them and ask them for help. They invite her friends to the house and make things attractive for them. They encourage independence and let her take chances to grow and develop.

TRAIT AND FACTOR THEORY

The process of helping individuals to select an occupation originated with Frank Parsons's work in the early 1900s. As discussed earlier, Parsons (1909) wrote *Choosing a Vocation* in which he described a systematic approach to matching people and occupations. This systematic trait-factor approach was prominent in the field of career counseling from the 1920s through the 1950s. During this time, many interest inventories, aptitude tests, and personality inventories were developed to support this theory.

Parsons (1909) describes three broad factors in helping people choose a vocation:

1. *Gain Self-Understanding:* Assess the persons' interests, abilities, ambitions, resources, limitations, values, personality, achievements, and aptitudes.
2. *Obtain Knowledge About the World-of-Work:* Help the person gain factual knowledge of the requirements and conditions of success, advantages and disadvantages, compensation, opportunities, and prospects of various occupations.
3. *Integrate Information About Oneself and the World-of-Work:* Help the client to use true reasoning in understanding his or her place in relation to these two sets of data to make informed decisions about a variety of occupations.

The theory was based on extensive interviewing and assessment, then a matching of the characteristics of an individual and the characteristics required for successful job performance in a variety of occupations. Frederickson (1982) summed up the primary assumptions of the trait-factor approach:

1. Each individual has a unique pattern of traits that can be accurately and reliably measured.
2. Each occupation has a unique pattern of measurable trait requirements that are necessary in order to perform that occupation successfully in a number of settings.
3. It is possible to match the individual traits with the job traits.
4. The closer the match between individual traits and job requirement traits, the more productivity and satisfaction the person will have in that particular occupation (p. 18).

Process of Vocational Guidance

Parsons (1909) outlined the process of vocational guidance as follows.

Personal Data. A careful statement of the principal facts about the client can be obtained from the intake interview.

Self-Analysis. A self-examination, with the career counselor, highlights tendencies and interest that will affect vocational choice. Assessment is a critical element in diagnosing and developing a treatment plan for your clients. Blocher and Biggs (1983) defined assessment as the ability to know your client from an internal and external perspective. The assessment process is a way of recognizing each client in terms of her uniqueness. Assessment, if used properly, can greatly enhance the career counseling relationship. Seligman (1996) described the assessment process as "a collaboration between counselor and client in which both gain in knowledge and understanding while their working relationship is developed and helpful interventions are identified and implemented" (p. 85).

Person's Choice and Decision. The client makes a choice about an occupation based on the intake interview and subsequent assessments.

Counselor's Analysis. The career counselor analyzes the client's choice based on information gained in regard to personal data and self-analysis. In this analysis, the career counselor tries to assess if the client is being logical and realistic in her evaluation of how her traits and factors match.

Outlook of the Vocational Field. Client and counselor investigate occupational information about the client's vocational choice. Your clients have many options available to them in gathering information about the world-of-work.

Induction and Advice. The client uses logical reasoning to develop a plan for implementing his or her choice.

Helpfulness. The client is helped to fit into the chosen work.

Options for Gathering Information

Shadowing Workers. This method allows a client to become familiar with a particular worker's daily tasks, the worker's attitudes toward work, characteristics of the work, and opportunities for advancement.

Interviewing Workers. This allows a client to learn more about different types of work by interviewing workers about the occupations. In addition, it allows the client to make contacts in a variety of occupational fields.

Volunteering. The client can develop work-related skills and try out a variety of skills through volunteer work.

Print Materials. These provide the client an opportunity to learn more about occupations through a media approach. Print materials come in many forms, including publications, books, films, videos, workbooks, and work samples.

Career Information Systems. The client can use these to systematically learn about occupations, since the occupations are grouped by common factors.

APPLICATION OF THE MATCHING THEORIES

Following is a treatment plan developed for a client, and then a demonstration of how a career counselor, using the matching theories, would counsel with the client.

Goals

1. Help the client understand the relationship between the manner in which she was raised by her parents and her occupational interests.
2. Help the client understand aspects of her personality.
3. Assist the client in gathering information about self and the world-of-work.

Objectives

1. Explore the client's personality type.
2. Identify the congruence, differentiation, and consistency of the client's personality type.
3. Explore the client's vocational identity.
4. Describe the nature of the client's relationship with her parents.
5. Gather information about self and the world-of-work.

Interventions

1. Administer the Self-Directed Search.
2. Administer My Vocational Situation.
3. Help the client explore a variety of sources of occupational information.
4. Assign the client to complete a battery of assessment instruments.
5. Teach the client how to make a rational, logical decision.

Counseling Process

Objective 1: Explore the Client's Personality Type. Kathy comes armed to the next session with a copy of the Self-Directed Search that she has completed. She gives the copy to the counselor. The career counselor hands the booklet back to Kathy and says, "Tell me what you learned about yourself from completing this instrument, Kathy." By doing this, the career counselor emphasizes the fact that the client is responsible for her own learning and her own career development. Kathy tells the counselor that her interests are in the Social, Artistic, and Enterprising (SAE) areas, and not in the Conventional area. She agrees with this assessment of herself. She sees herself as a people person and as verbal, artistic, and persuasive. She also sees herself as not very organized and not very attentive to details. Using the Occupations Finder that accompanies the SDS, Kathy has identified the following occupations associated with an SAE code: counselor, social service aide, vocational-rehabilitation counselor, elementary teacher, elementary school counselor, and home economist. She is encouraged by the career counselor to also explore occupations with the codes SEA, ASE, and AES.

Objective 2: Identify the Congruence, Differentiation, and Consistency of the Client's Personality Type. Holland (1973) believes that career counselors can use the following criteria in assessing the client.

Congruence is the degree of fit between individual and environment. For example, Social types flourish in Social environments largely because the environment provides the rewards and opportunities a Social person needs to be satisfied. Congruency has a tremendous impact on the person's satisfaction in an occupation. Therefore, incongruency occurs when a person works in an environment that does not provide the rewards and opportunities the person needs to be satisfied. For example, a Realistic type person working in an Investigative environment would be very dissatisfied.

Consistency is the degree of relatedness between personality types or between environmental models. This consistency is the internal coherence of an individual's scores (first two letters) on the Self-Directed Search. For example, a person with a high Realistic score followed by an Investigative score should be more predictable than one with a high Realistic score followed by a Social score.

Differentiation is the degree to which the person or a work environment is well defined. Differentiation is a measure of the person's crystallization of interests. For example, a person who is highly differentiated will resemble a single type to the exclusion of the other five types. On the other hand, a person who is not highly differentiated will resemble many types, and an undifferentiated work environment will be characterized by an equal number of the six types.

COUNSELOR: Now that you have taken the SDS, let's take a look at your Holland code. What were your highest three scores?

CLIENT: My highest score was in Social, my second highest score was in Artistic, and my third highest score was in Enterprising.
COUNSELOR: According to your code, you will be most comfortable in a social setting. What types of settings have your previous jobs been in? (checking for congruency in jobs held in the past)

When you are talking with your client, it is important to listen in terms of the six personality types. As the client talks about specific experiences she has had or about certain jobs in the past, listen for factors that describe the fit between the person and the environment in which they are working or living.

COUNSELOR: How much of a difference was there between your first and second letters? (checking for consistency)
CLIENT: Not too much difference, only five points. My third score was twelve points less than my first score.
COUNSELOR: That means that you will be most comfortable working in Social type occupations, but also activities in which some artistic things will be done.

The career counselor is checking for differentiation in the client's scores. There is, however, little differentiation between her first two scores. This gives the career counselor some sense of the degree of clarity of the person's identity. From this information, the career counselor surmises that the client does not have a real clear sense of her interests, abilities, and goals.

The career counselor will also make a note of the type of personality the client has. Personality types are not only indicative of the most comfortable work settings in which the client may work, but also give the career counselor insight into the types of relationships the person has, as well as how the person makes decisions.

Objective 3: Explore the Client's Vocational Identity. Identity is the degree of clarity and stability of a person's identity or the identity of a work environment. The degree of identity is defined by how clear the person's picture is of his or her interests, goals, and talents. Similarly, identity of the work environment is evident when an organization or work environment has clear goals, tasks, and rewards that have been established over a long period of time.

Objective 4: Describe the Nature of the Client's Relationship with Her Parents. Based on the childhood environments described in Roe's theory, the career counselor can predict the most suitable occupations as an orientation either toward people or away from people. Roe (1972) believes that the type of parenting influences career choice, and states that "different qualities of early parent-child interaction would result in the development of different interests and, through that, of different occupational choices" (p. 71). The theory concentrates on the attitude of one's parents toward or away from the child. Roe suggests that the category of occupations a person chooses depends on the person's child-raising experiences (see Figure 9.1). For

Figure 9.1   Roe's circular matching scheme

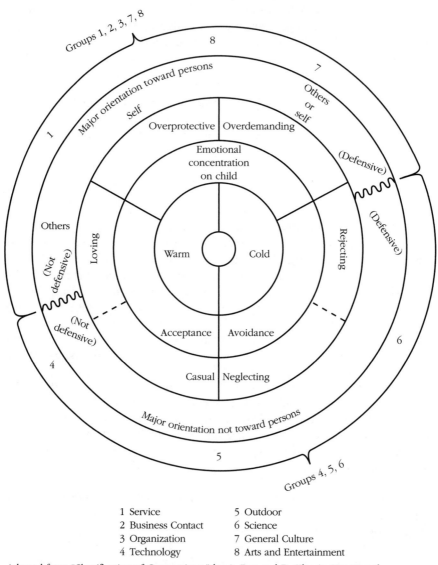

1 Service   5 Outdoor
2 Business Contact   6 Science
3 Organization   7 General Culture
4 Technology   8 Arts and Entertainment

Adapted from "Classification of Occupations," by A. Roe and D. Klos in *Vocational Development,* by J. H. Whitely and A. Resnikoff (Eds.), p. 213. Copyright © 1972, ACA. Reprinted with permission. No further reproduction authorized without written permission of the American Association for Counseling and Development.

example, people in Groups 1 (Service) and 8 (Arts and Entertainment) have a major orientation toward others; these people were brought up in homes that were either loving or overprotective (Service) or were overprotective or overdemanding (Arts and Entertainment). Conversely, people in Group 6 (Science) have a major orientation away from others; they were brought up in homes that were rejecting.

> COUNSELOR: Tell me a little about your parents.
> CLIENT: They were very good to me as a child. I have very pleasant memories of my childhood.
> COUNSELOR: Tell me more about some of your memories.
> CLIENT: Well, my mom and dad were always there for me. They were interested in my problems and in helping me to solve my problems. They were very caring and had my best interest in mind. They never punished me, but let me make mistakes and encouraged me to learn and grow from these mistakes.
> COUNSELOR: Do you have any negative memories?
> CLIENT: No, I can't think of any.

Objective 5: Gather Information About Self and the World-of-Work. We have already discussed a variety of methods that a career counselor can use to help clients explore information about themselves and the world-of-work. Many career counselors, working from a matching perspective, give their clients a battery of assessment instruments to gather information about the client's personality, values, interests, and aptitudes. In addition, clients should be helped to systematically explore the world-of-work.

> COUNSELOR: You have been gathering information about yourself. I feel like we have a pretty good idea of your interests, values, and aptitudes. Now let's look at some information about occupations that might help you decide on the best match for you. Let's start by developing a list of possible occupations you would like more information about. Then we will use a variety of resource materials to help you gather important information before you start making decisions about specific occupations.

CHAPTER 10

CONCEPTUALIZING DECISION-MAKING THEORIES

Decision-making theories suggest that although a person's career develops over time, there are certain points in each person's life when critical decisions occur. Some of these critical decisions include choosing a major in college, changing educational plans, looking for a job for the first time, changing jobs, quitting a job to start a small business, and contemplating retirement. Career counselors must be prepared to assist their clients in this complicated decision-making process. This approach to career counseling forms the fourth premise of an eclectic approach discussed in Chapter 1: *Most people do not possess a systematic, logical method for making career-related decisions. They often need to address the psychological traits related to their decision-making style and the barriers related to career decision making.* This chapter builds upon this premise by showing career counselors how to help clients make effective decisions, assess possible career alternatives, and examine stages of career decision making.

KATZ'S SEQUENTIAL ELIMINATION MODEL

Martin Katz (1966) first proposed a model of career decision making which states that clients must first examine their value system before considering alternative information and probabilities. Katz contends that career decision making is not a one-time event but rather a continual process involving one decision after another. Each decision influences not only subsequent decisions but also previously made decisions. Using self-concept as a major component in career development, Katz believes that an individual's value system affects his or her self-concept and thus is the major emphasis in career decision making. Katz suggests that the client who considers alternatives or probability of outcomes early in the career counseling process is not going to be effective.

A similar model has been proposed more recently (c.f., Gati, 1986; Gati, Fassa, & Houminer, 1995). This model, called the sequential elimination model, proposes that clients gradually eliminate alternatives that are not compatible with their desires. The career counselor uses the following nine steps to assist the client:

1. Define and structure the decision or problem.
2. Identify relevant aspects.
3. Evaluate and rank aspects by importance.
4. Identify optimal and acceptable levels of comfort with proposed solutions or alternatives.
5. Eliminate occupations incompatible with preferences.
6. Test sensitivity to changes in preferences.
7. Collect additional information.
8. Rank alternatives by overall desirability.
9. Outline steps to actualize the most preferred alternative.

This model can be especially effective when clients have multiple alternatives from which to choose.

TIEDEMAN'S CAREER DECISION-MAKING MODEL

Tiedeman and O'Hara (1963) postulate a vocational decision-making model of career development. Their model of career decision making places less emphasis on the occupations people choose and, instead, focuses on the way people make choices. The model recognizes a person's uniqueness and complexity and suggests that careers develop as experience helps individuals to differentiate and reintegrate an ego identity. This ego identity is influenced by the client's early childhood experiences within the family, his or her ability to resolve psychosocial crises, and the client's values compared with societal values. Their theory uses Erikson's theory of psychosocial development as its framework. Their work specifies a series of stages that clients go through over the life span.

Stages of Development

Anticipation. This stage consists of four phases. These four phases must be completed prior to entry into an occupation.

1. *Exploration:* This phase is a period of random behavior in which the individual interacts with the environment and receives feedback. It is characterized by collecting observations about the interaction and incorporation of information into an ego identity. Clients often imagine themselves in different situations, fantasize about occupations, and explore various vocational behaviors and

fears. The client's behavior in this phase is fairly unsystematic and random.

2. *Crystallization:* This period begins as these observations form patterns of behavior. In this phase, thoughts become orderly and stable.

3. *Choice:* The process of using self-observations to make tentative choices about occupations characterizes this phase. The advantages and disadvantages of choices form, and a preliminary choice begins to occur.

4. *Clarification:* This is the period of preparation for entry into an occupation. In this phase, the client often reassesses any choices made, and options are clarified.

If the client's choice is not appropriate, the process of exploration, crystallization, choice, and clarification begins again.

Implementation. This second stage consists of three phases concerning the implementation of and adjustment to an occupation by the client.

1. *Induction:* In this phase, the client implements her choice. If the client has chosen to further her education, the career counselor will want to explore anticipated changes in lifestyle and commitment needed to be successful. This period can also be the initial entry into a job. If this is the case, the person is primarily concerned with conforming to the organization.

2. *Reformation:* This period is signified when an individual is credible in the organization and can make changes that are necessary.

3. *Integration:* This period is defined when the individual and the organization are as one.

Tiedeman and O'Hara (1963) believe that individuals develop an ego identity through differentiation and integration. People differentiate themselves from their environment by observing their own behavior and that of others. This information is then integrated into their ego identity. More recently, Tiedeman and Miller-Tiedeman (1984) have defined another model based on the idea that how people view decision making is a function of how far they have advanced in their career. This is primarily measured in the language that people use in describing their careers. Two perspectives from which people describe their careers are personal reality and common reality. Personal reality is what feels right to the individual, as opposed to common reality, which is what is expected by other people. For example, a client may feel that she would be good at working with her hands, but others may expect the client to go to college and become a teacher.

Tiedeman (1988) also proposed the notion of Lifecareer. The Lifecareer notion states that an individual's life is his or her career and that people make decisions about how they construct or spend their lives. Specifically, the propositions of the theory include: Each person has a mission(s), purpose(s), reason(s) for being; each person evolves a theory of his or her own mission(s) and lives it while also making it more comprehensive; and there is no one way of doing things. Life unfolds differently for each person; each person is essentially a scientist applying and observing the results of moving to one's own inner wisdom; the whole of Lifecareer is greater than the sum of its individual parts; and Lifecareer works, not always the way one may desire, but it works (p. 34).

GELATT'S DECISION-MAKING MODEL

Gelatt (1962) presented an approach to career decision making that emphasized rationality. He believed that career decision making is a totally rational approach to making decisions that consists of defining objectives clearly, analyzing information rationally, predicting consequences, and being consistent in making a decision. Later in his career, Gelatt (1989) viewed career decision making from a much broader perspective and defined decision making as the "process of arranging and rearranging information into a course of action" (p. 253). He referred to this new decision-making strategy as "positive uncertainty." He believes that the following three steps comprise the decision-making process:

1. The information necessary to make an adequate decision must be obtained. This is a problem in society today, as new information becomes available all the time. Gelatt warns counselors to remember that information becomes obsolete almost as quickly as clients can gather it. The problem for the client then becomes how to process the massive amounts of information that he or she has gathered.
2. The next step is the process of arranging and rearranging information. Gelatt believes that discovering new goals during the process is as important as achieving the client's original goals, and that such skills as creativity, imagination, and reflection are at the heart of the decision-making process.
3. The choice in the career decision-making process now becomes one of combining both rational and intuitive thinking.

APPLICATION OF THE DECISION-MAKING THEORIES

Following is a treatment plan developed for a client, and then a demonstration of how a career counselor, using the decision-making theories, would counsel with the client.

Goals

1. Explore the way the client makes decisions.
2. Explore the factors that affect the client's decision-making ability.

Objectives

1. Explore the client's values and lifestyle as they relate to decision making.
2. Help the client identify possible occupational alternatives.
3. Help the client make a career decision.

Interventions

1. Administer a values inventory.
2. Help the client brainstorm occupational alternatives.
3. Discuss where the client is in the career decision-making process.
4. Have the client document how he/she has made decisions in the past.
5. Administer a decision-making inventory.
6. Teach the client a rational decision-making process.

Counseling Process

Objective 1: Explore the Client's Values and Lifestyle as They Relate to Decision Making. In the theories of career decision making, it is important that the client first learn more about his or her values system. This is accomplished by helping the client consider the influences that have come from family, friends, church, socioeconomic status, and any other factors that produce the client's value system. After the client better understands his or her value system, it is then time to begin viewing options and information. The career counselor should help the client identify options that offer a payoff that is most compatible with his or her values. Then, the likelihood of success in each option is considered.

Most of the career decision-making theories emphasize the importance of career decisions in light of the client's preferred lifestyle. Lifestyle preferences, however, are difficult to identify. Adler (1964) believes that one's lifestyle is a blueprint for living and a way of approaching important goals. Lifestyle develops as a function of the family constellation and early experiences within the family. Sharf (1997) states that an appropriate career choice is consistent with the person's lifestyle. In describing an Adlerian career counseling approach, he says that "an Adlerian counselor might help a client develop a feeling of confidence in his or her work and the ability to make a career choice" (p. 280).

Super's (1990) life-span, life-space theory of career development has brought to light the importance of incorporating dimensions of lifestyle such as job, leisure, membership in organizations, religion, home, and family. Zunker (1994) adds that lifestyle aspirations such as work climate, education, mobility, and financial security are also key factors in one's lifestyle orientation. Zunker (1994) developed the Dimensions of Life-Style Orientation Survey (DLOS) to assist people in identifying individual lifestyle dimensions. Zunker (1994) describes the following eleven dimensions of lifestyle that comprise the DLOS as important in career and life planning:

1. *Financial Orientation:* An orientation toward financial independence and social prominence
2. *Community-Involvement Orientation:* An orientation toward participation in community activities and community services
3. *Family Orientation:* An orientation toward family life
4. *Work-Achievement Orientation:* An orientation toward career development and commitment
5. *Work-Leadership Orientation:* An orientation toward a leadership role in the workplace
6. *Education Orientation:* An orientation toward self-improvement through educational attainment
7. *Structured Work-Environment Orientation:* An orientation toward regularly scheduled work hours
8. *Leisure Orientation:* An orientation toward leisure activities
9. *Mobility Orientation:* An orientation toward diversification and change
10. *Moderate-Secure Orientation:* An orientation toward moderation
11. *Outdoor-Work-Leisure Orientation:* An orientation toward work and leisure activities in the out-of-doors

By comparing lifestyle factors with other individual characteristics such as skills, interests, and values, career counselors can help the client in identifying congruent occupations. By allowing clients time to process their priorities in terms of desired lifestyle, the career counselor can help clients make important career decisions. Dillard (1985) suggests that by ignoring lifestyle factors, clients often limit their achievement. He contends that "successful career planning hinges on how well you integrate your way of life with the options which are open to you" (p. 10). Zunker (1994) adds that "a summary of lifestyle dimensions also provides an index to overall lifestyle preferences that focuses on important considerations in career life planning" (p. 90). Thus, lifestyle factors are critical in helping clients set priorities and goals for their career development.

COUNSELOR: Looking at these eleven different dimensions of lifestyle, talk to me about which ones seem most important to you.

CLIENT: First, family is extremely important. I also like a structured work environment. I don't want a job where I'm not sure what the hours are . . . or one where I'm working on a commission basis.

COUNSELOR: So you want a job where you have some control over the hours you work each week, or maybe even a part-time job. Anything else?

CLIENT: I guess mobility. I like a lot of diversity and change in my life and in my work.

COUNSELOR: O.k. So you want a job with many different activities going on each day. Are there any that you don't particularly need?

CLIENT: Financial for sure. I'm not out to make a lot of money. I just want to live comfortably, and help others.

COUNSELOR: So helping others is more important to you than money, Kathy? Any others that are not important?

Objective 2: Help the Client Identify Possible Occupational Alternatives.
Gelatt sees the major function of career counseling to be that of turning potentialities into realities by building decision-making skills. He believes decision making is a series of decisions in which each one influences subsequent decisions as well as those decisions made in the past. Gelatt sees the decision-making process as a three-step course of action: the client must first assess all of the possible alternative actions, the possible outcomes, and the probabilities; then the client uses his or her value system as a means of weighing the desirability of different outcomes; and finally the client finds a way to integrate and make a decision about the most appropriate action.

COUNSELOR: Kathy, what are some of the possible career alternatives available to you right now?

CLIENT: After gathering occupational information, I have identified about seven occupations that still interest me . . . college teaching, child care, art instructor, counselor, art therapist, social worker, and elementary school guidance counselor.

COUNSELOR: What would you say are the possible outcomes and the probabilities of each of these alternatives?

CLIENT: Well, I would say that all of them are possible. Based on my research, however, college teaching is the least probable because it would require at least a master's degree and probably a doctoral degree. I also would eliminate child care. I don't think I want to take care of small children. I also don't think I like art enough to be an art instructor for a living.

Objective 3: Help the Client Make a Career Decision. The career counselor's job is to assist the client in the systematic attainment of self and occupational information, and then to integrate this information in the form of a rational decision.

> COUNSELOR: O.k., Kathy, very good! Now let's take the remaining three alternatives and rank order them by compatibility with your values and by overall desirability.
>
> CLIENT: I think I would weigh them as follows: counseling, social work, and elementary school guidance counselor.
>
> COUNSELOR: O.k., I will now ask you to use your value system as a means of weighing the desirability of different outcomes. Let's see, you value family, work with kids, control over your hours, diversity, and helping others. (summarizing the previous conversation to highlight Kathy's values and lifestyle needs)
>
> CLIENT: That's right. All the jobs seem to match my value system.
>
> COUNSELOR: Let's eliminate any that don't. Do they all really match your values?
>
> CLIENT: Well, I guess social work doesn't. The others seem to.
>
> COUNSELOR: O.k., then . . . let's rank them according to your desirability at this time.
>
> CLIENT: I would say that elementary school guidance counseling would be the best match. I would have summers off to be with my family; I would have control over my hours; and I could still be a mentor to young people.
>
> COUNSELOR: O.k., Kathy, it seems as if you have made a career decision to go into the school guidance profession at this time. Now you will need to integrate all information and make a decision about the most appropriate action to implement your decision.

Notice how the career counselor helps the client to implement a systematic, logical method for making career-related decisions. He is also able to address barriers related to career decision making.

CHAPTER 11

CONCEPTUALIZING IMPLEMENTATION AND ADJUSTMENT THEORIES

Career choice is often the focus of a session for career counselors. However, implementing and adjusting to a career is also a critical part of the counseling process that career counselors address. This approach to career counseling forms the fifth premise of an eclectic approach discussed in Chapter 1: *All people experience, or hope to experience, intrapersonal and interpersonal satisfaction from the work they do. The better the match between a person and the occupation, the more the person will experience life satisfaction.* This chapter builds upon this premise by showing career counselors how to help clients adjust to work, help clients understand the interaction between the domains of the individual and the work setting, and help clients fuse their work and leisure.

LIPTAK'S LEISURE THEORY OF CAREER DEVELOPMENT

John Liptak (1998) drew upon the earlier work of Maslow's (1968) theory of motivation, principles in the transpersonal psychology literature, as well as Bordin's (1990) psychodynamic model of career choice in the development of the leisure theory of career development (LTCD). Bordin was one of the first career counselors to emphasize play in his theory of career selection. For Bordin, play was an important activity that brings joy and satisfaction. Bordin believed that play or the experience of joy that comes from play is highly sought after by all people at most times during their lives. Whenever possible, according to Bordin, people will seek to get joy from their work. It is this desire for satisfaction in work that leads people to select an occupation.

The leisure theory of career development states that the focus of career counseling should be on the client's leisure activities as well as his or her work experiences in order to help the client achieve true life satisfaction. Specifically, it addresses the question of why people express preference for different occupational and leisure activities at different points in their lives and how their decisions about work and leisure are related to their life satisfaction. The following are principles from the leisure theory of career development.

Leisure and Career Development

Career is comprised of the interaction and culmination of work and leisure roles. The work role accounts for all paid employment. The leisure role is comprised of all other activities including recreational activities, hobbies, learning, volunteering, self-maintenance, and family activities.

The theory suggests that career counselors should expand their notion of career to include the close synthesis between work and leisure concepts in career counseling. The study of the effects of leisure on work can be traced back to Super's (1940) study of the psychology of avocations. In his study, model railroaders, amateur photographers, and amateur symphony orchestras were found to be engaging in their hobbies in one of three ways: (1) as extensions of their occupations, (2) as compensation for their occupations, or (3) as unrelated to their occupations.

As changes have taken place in society and the world-of-work, career counselors are recognizing the inclusion of leisure as an integral component of a career (c.f., Bloland & Edwards, 1981; Bolles, 1988; Liptak, 1990, 1991a, 1992a; McDaniels, 1984, 1989; Super, 1980) and have suggested that career counseling be expanded to include all aspects of one's life. Miller (1999) also cites literature calling for a redefinition of career (c.f., Mirvis & Hall, 1994). She states that "evolving definitions encompass elements beyond work experience" (p. 9). Thus, career counselors need to be more aware of leisure and the effect it has on a client's career.

Variations in Leisure Activities in Different Stages of Development

All people engage in leisure activities because these activities allow them to be interactive, spontaneous, creative, and playful. The types of leisure activities in which people engage, the amount of time spent engaging in these activities, and thus the contexts vary with the stages of their life development.

In early childhood (ages 2–5), one's parents are the major influence in one's life. The person develops a capacity for play and imagination and develops communication skills. It is at this point also that the person develops a sense of right and wrong.

In middle childhood (ages 6–12), the person's schooling is the major influence. During this period, the person learns to relate to social peers at school and at after-school activities and develops close friendships. Physical, intellectual, and psychological dimensions and capabilities also grow during this period. The person's eye-hand coordination increases, and manual dexterity is developed. At this point the person begins to learn about his or her interests and abilities through leisure. The person also learns new motor skills, and cognitive abilities develop.

In adolescence (ages 13–18), the person continues to explore and become aware of new leisure activities. Kleibert, Larson, and Csikszentmihalyi (1986) found that leisure activities during this period of life help people to acquire the necessary skills to handle the demands of adult leisure options. School continues to be the primary context for the person's leisure experiences. The family, however, provides an opportunity to explore activities not experienced in school. This time is comprised of both team and individual leisure experiences. All these experiences allow the person to refine his or her likes and dislikes. At this point, the person also learns how to relate leisure activities to occupations and coursework in postsecondary schools.

In young adulthood (ages 19–25), the person has more freedom in making choices about how to spend his or her leisure time. At this point, education becomes a leisure choice, not a requirement, for the person. This stage is a time for taking risks and exploring a variety of options related to the person's leisure activities. The work setting or postsecondary school is now the major influence in the person's life. For those seeking additional education, leisure activities most likely evolve around the classroom setting, while those seeking employment may use leisure to learn additional vocational skills or to try out new vocations.

In adulthood (ages 26–45), the person is probably working part- or full-time. The person's job often dictates the types of leisure experiences in which the person engages. For example, a computer programmer may spend his time reading about new computer programs. Or if the person gets married and starts a family, leisure activities may revolve around the family.

In midlife (ages 46–65), leisure often replaces work as the person's major source of life satisfaction. At this point, leisure may bring new meaning to the person's life. The person may begin to feel his job is too stressful, dull, or not fulfilling his needs. He may choose to volunteer his services and expertise, thus using leisure experiences to pass on his knowledge to others. At this stage of life, the individual also has more time for leisure activities because his children are typically older or have already left home. Similarly, he has more time and money to devote to leisure. He also prepares financially and psychologically for retirement and then begins to cut back on work.

In laterlife (age 65+), the person engages primarily in leisure activities. She has a tremendous amount of time now to devote to her leisure interests. Although fewer people are retiring at age 65, many cut back on the number of hours they work, thus increasing the number of leisure hours available to them. Leisure activities can provide alternative uses of time for the person.

Crystallization of Personal Characteristics in Leisure Activities

People are genetically endowed and exhibit different interests, abilities, values, and personality characteristics. Although the crystallization of some of these characteristics occurs during work, most of these unique characteristics are crystallized primarily through participation in leisure activities.

In his study of the interaction between work and leisure over a person's life span (c.f., Liptak, 1991b, 1991c, 1992b), Liptak (1991b) found that leisure can actually play a more important role in career development than work. Similarly, Rogers and Sawyers (1988) believe that leisure has a tremendous effect on a person's social, emotional, and cognitive development. This research indicates that leisure provides people with an opportunity to: practice new skills; explore occupations; try out occupations; gain new skills; experience events; unite mind, body, and spirit; transform reality into symbolic representations of the world; consolidate previous learning; experience peak moments; explore problem-solving styles; and develop creative and aesthetic appreciation.

Career and Needs Satisfaction

People are constantly evolving toward self-actualization and self-transcendence. During this evolution, people are motivated to satisfy or fulfill their needs through work and leisure.

Maslow (1971) suggests that people have inner drives or needs that motivate them. He identifies a basic needs structure comprised of five levels of needs—physiological, safety, belongingness and love, esteem, and self-actualization—that are arranged in a hierarchy proceeding from lower-level needs to higher-level needs (see Figure 11.1). A person is motivated to proceed through each of these needs one at a time. This progression is the growth process for an individual's life.

Matching Characteristics of Individuals and Their Work

A person's ability to fulfill his or her needs at work, and thus experience increased job satisfaction, depends on the quality of the match between the individual's characteristics and the characteristics of the work.

The more people are able to fulfill their needs at work, the less they need to rely on leisure activities for life satisfaction. For example, a person who loves being a secretary not only makes enough money to fulfill physiological and security needs but also fulfills needs for belongingness, esteem, and possibly self-actualization.

Figure 11.1   Maslow's hierarchy of needs

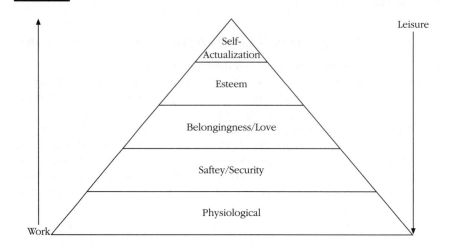

Career and Life Satisfaction

Life satisfaction is the goal of all people. Life satisfaction is comprised of work satisfaction and leisure satisfaction.

Pearson (1998) completed a study to determine if job satisfaction and leisure satisfaction are predictors of psychological health. He found that job satisfaction and leisure satisfaction both had high correlations with psychological health, but low correlations with each other. Consequently, he contended that "the combination of job satisfaction and leisure satisfaction was a stronger predictor of psychological health than job satisfaction alone" (pp. 421–422). Thus, participants of the study who were more satisfied in both work and leisure tended to have greater levels of psychological health. Leisure, therefore, "adds something to psychological health not accounted for by one's job" (p. 423).

From this study support was found for the leisure compensation theory (Staines, 1980), which suggests that people who are dissatisfied at work can compensate for this dissatisfaction through leisure experiences that satisfy the needs not being met on the job. Therefore, Pearson (1998) concludes that career counselors are often compelled to help a client find a more satisfying job or occupation rather than help the client find more satisfying leisure activities. He states that for some clients, the cost of making a job change is too great and that changes in leisure are often more feasible. "Accordingly, instead of thinking narrowly in terms of increasing job satisfaction, the career counselor might be more successful in improving clients' well-being by encouraging his participation in more fulfilling leisure activities" (p. 423).

Reliance on Leisure for Life Satisfaction

Because not all people are able to satisfy their needs at work, leisure often becomes the vehicle for attaining life satisfaction. The more people are unable to satisfy their needs at work, the more they must rely on leisure activities for their life satisfaction.

Many career development theorists (i.e., Dawis, 1992; Dawis, England, & Lofquist, 1964; Dawis & Lofquist, 1984; Hoppock, 1976) have proposed the notion that occupations are chosen to meet needs. Liptak (1998) believes this to a certain extent, but acknowledges that not all clients are able to meet their needs through the work they do. For example, an individual may have to take a job as a secretary to feed his family but only be able to meet his physiological needs at this job. Career counselors too often assume that all people want to or are able to meet all of their needs at work. Many clients will be able to satisfy their needs through leisure activities. The career counselor must have a working knowledge of leisure counseling techniques to provide this assistance (Liptak, 1991c).

Career Decision Making

There is a direct correlation between a person's ability to satisfy needs and his or her life satisfaction. Therefore, a person's career can be seen as a series of decisions through which an individual strives to identify work and leisure activities in which he or she can find joy and satisfy his or her needs.

The desired outcome of career counseling with the leisure theory of career development is the greater realization of a client's potentials as a human being. Maslow (1968) has suggested that the lack of attainment of lower-level needs can motivate people to correct their situation (deficiency motivation). On the other hand, humans are also motivated by the potentialities of growth itself, or the incentive to make actual what we feel is latent within us (growth motivation). (See Figure 11.2.)

Much of career counseling is geared toward the level of need deficiency the client is experiencing. Career counselors may be concerned with helping the client to fulfill his deficiency motivation through such activities as finding a job, increasing the client's self-esteem, or helping him return to school. On the other hand, career counselors often work with clients to fulfill their growth motivation. Growth motivation goals include spiritual growth, self-actualization, and transcendence; these goals are accomplished through the realization of one's true self and one's purpose in life. Therefore, the objective of growth motivation is to help the client develop a rich and meaningful life.

Left- and Right-Brain Methods of Career Choice

Due to the complexity and ambiguity of the career decision-making process, career choice is often an affective right-brain process as much as it is a cognitive left-brain process.

Figure 11.2   Maslow's growth-deficiency motivation theory

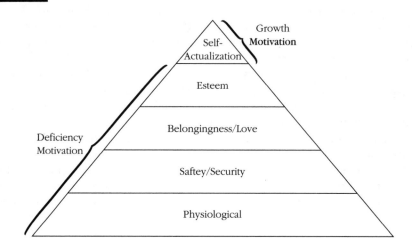

Career choice is not always a logical, linear process. Career counseling, however, has always relied on a systematic decision-making process. In this process, the decision maker identifies the decision to be made, gathers information, identifies appropriate options, and eliminates options until there is one best option available. Rather than relying solely on this traditional "left-brain" model, the leisure theory of career development also recognizes the importance of the intuitive "right-brain" methods for arriving at career decisions.

A person's intuitive mind is nonverbal and operates through pictures, symbols, inspirations, and metaphors. Jung (1923) described intuition as direct knowing or learning of something without the conscious use of reasoning—gaining immediate apprehension or understanding. Vaughan (1979) believes that "the role of intuition in creativity, problem-solving, and interpersonal relationships is vital" (p. 3). Similarly, Emery (1994) writes that intuition is a hunch, gut feeling, or sudden insight that impels decision makers to take action, go into new endeavors, and retrieve innovative solutions to all types of problems, including career-related problems.

Left-brain exploration activities focus on assessment and gathering information about the world-of-work through career exploration, vocational tryout, and use of technology to retrieve occupational information. Right-brain career counseling techniques are often useful in helping people achieve their transcendence needs. Some of these techniques include meditation of "Who am I?" (Novak, 1989), creative visualization (Gawain, 1978), the use of intuition (Day, 1996), handwriting analysis, past-life regression, dream work, fantasizing, and other-hand writing.

Fusing Work and Leisure

Job satisfaction, achievement, and stability in an occupation depend on how successful a person is at finding work that allows that person to be spontaneous and creative by fusing his or her work and leisure activities.

Liptak (1998) believes that the ultimate goal of career counseling is to facilitate the client's fusion of work and leisure. He says that the fusion of work and leisure is a way of helping people to attain self-actualization and life satisfaction. People who are successful in fusing their work and leisure activities find a sense of playfulness at work, experience many peak moments in doing their work, feel a sense of spontaneity and creativity, and are motivated to master their daily work activities.

Some people are fortunate enough to be able to satisfy all their needs from physiological to self-actualization needs at work. For these people, work is a source of tremendous life satisfaction. It is almost as though these people are unable to easily separate work and leisure activities. Work, in this case, provides a forum where employees can be spontaneous, creative, and playful. For example, the individual who teaches elementary school during the day and in the evening spends a great deal of time tutoring, taking classes to further his education, and developing curricular materials for the school district where he teaches receives tremendous life satisfaction from teaching. There is a fusion between this person's work and leisure activities. Athletes are another group of individuals who often fuse work and leisure activities and who experience real life satisfaction. All people are able to experience this fusion.

Maslow (1968) also believed that work and play can be transcended into one. He called these moments peak experiences. Similarly, Csikszentmihalyi (1990) wrote about flow, or about how we find happiness. He believes that happiness is a side effect and not achieved when directly pursued. He refers to this flow as the psychology of optimal experience. These are times when the person forgets about the passage of time because he is completely absorbed in what he is doing. Csikszentmihalyi concludes that the more time people spend in this absorbed state, the happier they are. He believes that in order to achieve this flow, the person must have a goal or challenge, total involvement or immersion, and concentration without self-consciousness. Career counselors must find ways to help people progress through lower-need levels and live at higher-need levels.

THEORY OF WORK ADJUSTMENT (TWA)

The theory of work adjustment (Dawis, 1992; Dawis, England, & Lofquist, 1964; Dawis & Lofquist, 1984) assumes that an individual has certain requirements for survival and wellness that are satisfied primarily through the environment. These requirements or needs can be divided into two categories: biological needs for survival, and psychological needs for wellness. Reinforcers are available in the environment that maintain or increase the rate of the specified behavior. The TWA assumes that workers have work needs that can be satisfied by the work environment and can be maintained through the use of work reinforcers such as pay and benefits. The work environment, likewise, has requirements that can be satisfied through the completion of the task requirements or the job of the worker. When both entities have met each other's requirements, both are said to be satisfied. Therefore, the primary factor in work adjustment is the match between the expectations of the employee and the expectations of the organization.

Dawis, England, and Lofquist (1964) developed a number of propositions in their theory of work adjustment including:

1. Work adjustment is composed of satisfactoriness (success) and satisfaction.
2. Satisfactoriness is determined by the relationship of the individual's abilities and the requirements of the workplace, assuming the individual's needs are being met by the organization's reward system.
3. Satisfaction is determined by how well the reward system of the organization meets the individual's needs, assuming the individual's skills meet the organization's requirements.
4. Satisfaction and satisfactoriness have moderating effects on each other.
5. Tenure in the job is a function of satisfactoriness and satisfaction.
6. The fit between the individual's needs and skills and the environment requirements and rewards increases as a function of tenure.

These propositions can be used as a guide for the career counseling process. People are motivated to fulfill work requirements and to have their personal requirements fulfilled by work. Work adjustment is the effort of the individual to maintain this correspondence. The career counselor at this point helps the client evaluate the fit between her skills and needs and those of each of the jobs. To do so, Dawis and Lofquist (1984) believe that the focus of counseling is on value and ability assessment. They believe that interests are an expression of abilities and values. To assess values, they developed the Minnesota Importance Questionnaire (MIQ; Rounds, Henly, Dawis, Lofquist, & Weiss, 1981) to measure worker needs. To assess abilities, they use the General Aptitude Test Battery (GATB; U.S. Department of Labor, 1982), which measures predicted skills.

Just as there are measures that can be used to measure an individual's abilities and values, there are similar measures for abilities and values needed for occupations. For example, the Occupational Ability Patterns (OAP) utilized on the GATB and the Minnesota Job Description Questionnaire (MJDQ; Borgen, Weiss, Tinsley, Dawis, & Lofquist, 1968) assess how well an occupation meets a worker's needs.

HERSHENSON'S MODEL OF WORK ADJUSTMENT

Hershenson's model (Hershenson, 1974, 1981) advocates that work adjustment is the result of the complex interaction among three domains for the person and her work environment. Hershenson (1996) says that although most people make multiple career choices over their life span, they spend more time working at an occupation than they spend making career choices. He says that "the issues involved in working at an occupation, however, have received disproportionately little attention in career counseling theory and practice" (p. 442). Changes in any one of the domains usually precipitate changes in the other domains. Hershenson (1996) contends that work adjustment involves the interaction between the domains in the individual and the work setting.

As can be seen in Figure 11.3, the three domains for an individual include:

Figure 11.3   Hershenson's model of work adjustment

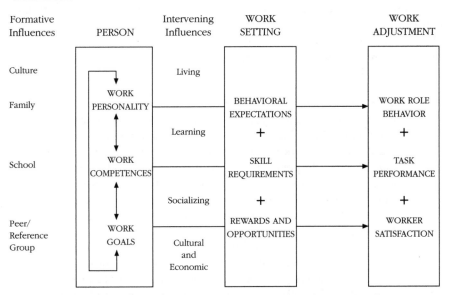

From "Work Adjustment: A Neglected Area in Career Counseling," by D. B. Hershenson, *Journal of Counseling & Development,* May/June 1996, vol. 74, pp. 442–446.

1. *Work Personality:* This develops during the preschool years and consists of the person's self-concept as a worker, the person's system of work motivation, and the person's work-related needs and values.
2. *Work Competencies:* These develop during the school years and consist of work habits, physical and mental skills applicable in work, and interpersonal skills applicable in the work setting.
3. *Work Goals:* These develop as the person prepares to leave school and enter the work world and are consistent with the person's work personality and work competencies.

Similarly, the three domains for the work setting (see Figure 11.3) include:

1. Organizational culture and behavioral expectations
2. Job demands and skill requirements
3. Internal and external rewards for the worker

In addition, opportunities available to the worker are critical.

Hershenson (1996) says that in counseling for work adjustment, the career counselor needs to focus on the relationship between the person and the work setting. This relationship can present problems in the client's work role behavior, task performance, or worker satisfaction. "In examining this relationship, the counselor and client must also come to understand the effects of the intervening systems of living, learning, and socialization on this relationship, and the effects of the cultural and economic context on all the constituent elements including their effects on the counselor's perceptions and practices" (p. 443). Therefore, counseling for work adjustment consists of making interventions on any one or any combination of the following domains (see Figure 11.3):

1. Work role behavior is acting appropriately to one's position in the work setting, which is primarily related to work personality in the person and the behavioral expectations of the work setting. Problems with work role behavior will be exhibited in such behaviors as poor interpersonal relationships with coworkers, arguing with customers, or not taking adequate initiative on the job. The career counselor needs to look at the client's work personality compared with the organizational climate and expectations of the organization.
2. Task performance involves the quality and quantity of one's work output, which is primarily related to work competencies in the person and the skill requirements of the work setting. In problems with task performance, the career counselor needs to examine the client's competencies in terms of the work being produced as they relate to the job demands and skills needed on the job.

3. Worker satisfaction involves gratification resulting from one's work. If clients are not satisfied at work, the career counselor needs to look at the client's values and work goals as they relate to the rewards and opportunities in the work setting.

APPLICATION OF THE IMPLEMENTATION AND ADJUSTMENT THEORIES

Following is a treatment plan developed for a client, and then a demonstration of how a career counselor, using the implementation and adjustment theories, would counsel with the client.

Goals

1. Help the client examine her life satisfaction.
2. Explore how the client's needs are being met at work.
3. Increase the client's knowledge of the effects of leisure upon career.

Objectives

1. Explore the client's work personality and work competencies.
2. Explore the client's life satisfaction.
3. Identify activities to meet the client's needs.
4. Assess the client's work adjustment style.
5. Explore the client's barriers to employment success.

Interventions

1. Administer the Career Exploration Inventory and the Leisure/Work Search Inventory.
2. Assist the client in identifying satisfying leisure activities.
3. Explore the rewards and opportunities available to the client at work.
4. Discuss the job demands and skills requirements of various occupations.
5. Explore the relationship between the client's work and leisure activities.
6. Administer the Job Search Attitudes Inventory and the Barriers to Employment Success Inventory.
7. Utilize right-brain career counseling techniques.

Counseling Process

Objective 1: Explore the Client's Work Personality and Work Competencies. Satisfaction, according to the TWA, is based on an evaluation of how well the client's capabilities are met through work. These capabilities that predict the success of workers include such things as skills, values, aptitudes, and personality.

In providing career counseling, the client and counselor must make evaluations based on premises about the occupations and the client. To do so, the following steps are conducted:

1. Assess the client.
2. Assess the work environment.
3. Ascertain correspondence between them.

When counseling dissatisfied clients, the career counselor should be sure to check on the client's expectations of the job versus the expectations of the organization. The career counselor needs to make sure that the client has expectations of receiving from the organization the following dimensions: a sense of meaning or purpose in the job; personal development opportunities; interesting work; challenging work; responsibility in the job; recognition for good work; prestige in the job; friendly coworkers; structure in the environment; security in the job; advancement opportunities; and feedback from the supervisor. The lack of any of these dimensions can upset the balance and cause dissatisfaction and unsatisfactoriness.

The career counselor uses tests that have been administered previously. If no assessment data are available, the career counselor would administer such assessment instruments as the Career Exploration Inventory for interests, the General Aptitude Test Battery for aptitudes, the Work Values Inventory for values, the Myers-Briggs Type Indicator for personality, and the Leisure/Work Search Inventory for leisure interests. The career counselor should help the client examine the match between her values and lifestyle preferences and occupations of interest. For example, Kathy values children, autonomy, and creativity. As an elementary teacher, Kathy could work with young children, while simultaneously designing lessons and materials that enable her to utilize her creativity and autonomy.

If the client does not have enough information to match her values and lifestyle preferences with an occupation, then the career counselor would direct her to different types of career resources. Clients need sufficient information about the work organization as well as knowledge about themselves. Satisfaction and success in the occupation depend on the person/ environment fit.

Objective 2: Explore the Client's Life Satisfaction. People who come to career counseling do so because they are unable to fulfill their needs and are thus dissatisfied with life. As was illustrated with the leisure theory of career development, (LTCD), life satisfaction is comprised of work satisfaction and leisure satisfaction. A client's failure to fulfill his needs in either work or leisure causes life dissatisfaction. Career counselors can use Maslow's needs theory in helping clients identify their level of life satisfaction.

COUNSELOR: Kathy, let's talk about your life satisfaction. How satisfied would you say that you are with your life?
CLIENT: I think that I'm pretty satisfied.
COUNSELOR: Are your physiological needs—for example, food, air, and water—being met?
CLIENT: Yes, they are.
COUNSELOR: How about your safety and security needs?
CLIENT: Yes, I believe so. I feel like we make enough money to be comfortable. I also feel secure in my relationships.
COUNSELOR: What about your belongingness and love needs?
CLIENT: Yes, between my husband, daughter, parents, and friends . . . I feel both love and belongingness.
COUNSELOR: How about your esteem needs?
CLIENT: Well, I feel pretty good about myself. I could feel better though.

At this point, the career counselor has proceeded through Maslow's hierarchy from the lowest, most basic needs to higher-level needs. Esteem seems to be the place in the hierarchy where Kathy's needs are not being met. She appears to have a lot of self-confidence but is not getting much self-esteem from her job. A counselor, using the LTCD, could approach this problem in two ways: by helping the client identify more satisfying work related to her personal characteristics, and by helping her identify fulfilling leisure activities.

Objective 3: Identify Activities to Meet the Client's Needs. Like trait-factor counselors who use the classic matching model, career counselors using the LTCD believe that clients can attain life satisfaction through leisure even if they do not have job satisfaction. Liptak developed several assessment instruments to gather information about the client's leisure interests. The Career Exploration Inventory (CEI; Liptak, 1992b) and the Leisure/Work Search Inventory (LSI; Liptak, 1994b) were developed to address the need for quality leisure assessment instruments that would enable individuals to systematically explore their leisure interests. The CEI is a self-scoring and self-interpreting interest inventory that measures a client's interests in work, leisure, and learning. It utilizes a developmental approach that measures interests from the past, those in the present, and those anticipated in the future. The LSI measures an individual's interests in order to help her turn these interests into possible employment opportunities in a full- or part-time job, small-business enterprise, or home-based business.

COUNSELOR: Looking at your results from the CEI and LSI, it appears as if you have a lot of interest in artistic activities. Tell me where your interest and aptitude for art comes from.

CLIENT: I'm not sure. I have always enjoyed drawing and sketching in my spare time. I like to draw animals and figures from scratch.

COUNSELOR: Have you ever thought about what other types of leisure activities you either have interest in or might like to do in the future? Let's look at the results of your Career Exploration Inventory. According to the CEI, you also have an interest in writing, plants and animals, and human services.

CLIENT: Well, again, I like to draw and write, take care of plants, and help my little girl with her homework.

COUNSELOR: Have you thought about writing and/or illustrating books, maybe children's books, in your spare time?

CLIENT: No, I haven't, but it is an interesting thought!

The career counselor helps Kathy identify some things she might like to do or continue doing in her spare time. Some of these leisure-time activities may also lead to other types of jobs or small-business opportunities.

Objective 4: Assess the Client's Work Adjustment Style. Dawis and Lofquist (1984) describe several work adjustment styles. These styles include:

1. *Flexibility:* The degree to which individuals will tolerate a lack of congruence between their work environment and their personal environment
2. *Perseverance:* How long an individual is willing to stay in an environment that does not fit
3. *Activeness:* The degree to which an individual will try to alter the work environment to increase correspondence with a person's personal style
4. *Reactiveness:* The degree to which an individual is willing to change his work personality to fit the work environment

It is important for the career counselor to assess each client's work adjustment style. Some clients will be able to persevere at work if they are able to engage in leisure activities that provide some measure of self-esteem, a sense of belongingness, and some self-actualization. Other clients will have little perseverance and will be more actively searching for a different type of work. The career counselor must be prepared to work with these clients in finding a new job immediately. That is why career counselors must be knowledgeable in job search methods and in barriers that are keeping their clients from enjoying success at work.

Objective 5: Explore the Client's Barriers to Employment Success. Career counselors need to help clients explore barriers to the implementation of their career choices. Several assessment instruments have been developed to help clients explore barriers to their success in the workplace. The Barriers to Employment Success Inventory (BESI; Liptak, 1996) was designed to help clients identify the major barriers to obtaining a job or succeeding in their employment. The BESI yields a raw score in five major category clusters including Personal and Financial, Emotional and Physical, Career Decision-Making and Planning, Job Seeking Knowledge, and Training and Education. In addition, Liptak (1994) developed the Job Search Attitudes Inventory (JSAI), which was designed to make job seekers more aware of their self-directed and other-directed attitudes about the search for employment.

 PART FOUR

INTEGRATING THE THEORIES

CHAPTER 12

APPLICATION OF THE TREATMENT PLANNING MODEL

Depending on the client and his or her concerns, the career counseling process for most clients extends over several sessions. In this model of treatment planning, the theories of career development are used to understand human behavior and make diagnoses about your clients. Therefore, as a career counselor, you analyze the data you have gathered through the lens of the theories of career development. It is within these theories that you will search for ideas to help you and your client identify goals for counseling and resolve problems. You are thus analyzing the data you gather in the intake interview through each of the five categories of theories.

The developmental theories can be helpful in gathering information about the person's background, growth, development, and home and school environments. This information has helped to forge the person's identity. Information about the person's life span and life space will help you understand the lifestyle and value structure that has influenced the person's choices.

The cognitive theories help us to understand the client's thought processes and how he or she processes information. These theories provide us with information from a cognitive perspective about the underlying reasons for career problems. Identifying a client's irrational beliefs and providing sound information can help clients make better informed career decisions.

The matching theories are helpful in identifying the match between factors of the work environment and traits of the worker. These theories stress the importance of our client's need for information about himself and the world-of-work. Equipped with this information, clients are able to make rational decisions about their careers.

The decision-making theories provide us with possible models to use in explaining and outlining the decision-making process to our clients. These theories examine the process that leads up to our clients making a career choice.

The implementation and adjustment theories are useful in describing and exploring what happens once a person has made a career decision. These theories help us explain and remedy job adjustment problems and issues. They also show us alternatives for attaining life satisfaction in activities or interests other than work.

Therefore, during the process of career counseling, these five categories will be used in helping the client to set goals, identify objectives, and choose appropriate interventions. Most career counselors use a variety of techniques from each of the five theory categories in an eclectic approach. In working with Kathy or any client, I would approach counseling using an eclectic format. I would work toward an integration of concepts and techniques from the various theories of career development. Each of the five categories of theories of career development has something unique to offer in understanding and counseling your client.

I will attempt to demonstrate how I would use a combination of the five different approaches with a client that I recently had the opportunity to counsel. The client's name is Gary.

Case of Gary

Gary felt as though his life was over. He had worked for twenty-eight years at a small plant that manufactured parts for televisions. Ever since the slump in the electronics industry about five years before, there had been layoffs at his plant. But somehow he thought that he would always have a job because he had been at the plant for such a long time. His response was, "I have more seniority than most of the workers still remaining here." But then the plant manager came to Gary and told him that the plant would be closing in two months. Gary could not believe what he had heard.

A month later, Gary was still in shock. His first response was one of denial. He said such things as "Maybe it's a mistake, maybe it won't happen, or maybe someone else will buy the plant." As time went on, it began to dawn on him that the plant was really going to close. At 46, Gary was out of work for the first time since high school. He was scared. "What will I do now?" he kept asking. Gary ran a metal press at the plant and knew that his skills were not in great demand. "Nobody else will hire me. Where else can I work?" Some of Gary's coworkers at the plant were going to relocate to Florida to try and find work. Gary was not interested in this prospect. He and his family had lived in Philadelphia their entire lives. They did not want to move.

Gary came to my office and told me that he needed help finding a job. I told him that I was a career counselor and that I could help him develop a career/life plan. We made an appointment, and about three days later, Gary came to my office to begin our career counseling sessions. The first thing I had Gary do while he was waiting was to fill out the Career/Life Exploration Record. This gave me some background information and a guide for starting the intake interview.

The second part of the intake interview consists of gathering personal history information. For Gary, I was able to gather the following information:

Appearance
- Client was appropriately dressed in blue jeans and a sweatshirt
- He was clean, and his hair was washed
- Wore glasses
- Normal facial expressions and mannerisms

Behavior
- Client maintained good eye contact
- Seemed very open and cooperative
- Seemed anxious and a little depressed
- Showed no unusual behaviors

Speech
- Very articulate
- Spoke very slowly and deliberately

Emotions
- Said he has been depressed since hearing about being laid off
- Stated he was somewhat nervous about counseling
- Flat affect
- Seemed somewhat depressed

Orientation to Reality
- Good awareness of time, place, and persons
- Good awareness of his situation

Concentration and Attention
- Demonstrated ability to focus on stimuli and sustain attention
- Seemed alert and responsive

Thought Processes
- Demonstrated capacity for abstract thinking
- Showed no unusual thought processes

Thought Content
- Showed no suicidal ideation
- Showed no anger, violence, or aggression
- Showed no other prominent thoughts

Perception
- No unusual sensory experiences

Memory
- Showed adequacy of immediate, short-term, and long-term memory

Intelligence
- Demonstrated average intelligence

Judgment and Insight
- Demonstrated adequate decision-making and problem-solving ability
- Aware of strengths and weaknesses

Medical History
- Client stated he is in good health; reported being hospitalized at age 32 for gall bladder surgery; no other hospitalizations
- Reported no problems sleeping or eating
- Reported no significant allergies
- Reported no other illnesses

While completing the intake assessment, I try to utilize rapport-building interview skills. I use a lot of encouragers and call the client by name. I try to paraphrase his statements and reflect what he is feeling as often as possible. I occasionally summarize what he is saying just to make sure I understand completely what he is telling me. Much of what I did during the beginning phase of the counseling process was to provide support and encouragement to Gary. Because Gary had suffered a great loss in his life, he was still somewhat in shock. It was very important to build a relationship with Gary quickly so that he would feel comfortable as we moved to the middle phase of the career counseling process. I also was using the theories of career development to identify and clarify Gary's problems and goals. The future goals that Gary and I identified at the end of our initial counseling session are listed below:

1. Help the client learn more about his life-span issues.
2. Help the client learn more about his life-space issues.
3. Correct irrational and dysfunctional beliefs.
4. Gather realistic occupational information.
5. Help the client understand aspects of his personality.
6. Explore the way the client makes decisions.
7. Help the client examine his life satisfaction.
8. Increase knowledge of the effects of leisure upon career.

At the end of the first session, I sometimes assign clients homework to do for our next career counseling session. With Gary, however, I felt that this might be too much for him; I did not want him to get discouraged too quickly. The other area that I was concerned about and needed to discuss at the end of the first session was the extent of Gary's depression. I could have given him a depression scale; but because I did not feel that his depression was too severe and saw no suicide ideation, I recommended that he might want to see his medical doctor for a physical or possibly for antidepressant medication.

When Gary returned for his next appointment, we started the second session by working on one of his goals. Remember that goals help to keep the client and you on track in the session. Therefore, I recommended that we work on one of the developmental goals.

Goal 1: Help the Client Learn More About His Life-Span Issues.

Objectives
1. Assess the client's vocational identity and occupational self-concept.
2. Assess the client's vocational maturity.
3. Assess the client's career maturity.

Interventions
1. Identify developmental tasks related to the client's stage in the life span.
2. Ask the client to do a career autobiography.
3. Give the client a battery of assessment instruments.

As can be seen from the goals, I wanted to begin by helping Gary explore his life-span and life-space issues. To explore his life span, I had him talk to me about his life history after he completed a career autobiography or lifeline. Because he had not had a variety of occupational or educational experiences, he appeared to have limited vocational maturity. Gary appeared to be in the exploration developmental stage and had to resolve the crystallization developmental tasks. This meant that he had yet to formulate a general vocational goal because of a lack of awareness about his resources, interests, abilities, and values. In other words, he had yet to begin planning for a preferred occupation. I also started to show him how his leisure experiences may have impacted his life and career.

To identify his vocational identity and occupational self-concept, I had Gary complete a battery of assessment instruments including a values card sort, the Career Exploration Inventory (CEI), and the General Aptitude Test Battery (GATB). On the values card sort, Gary listed the following values as "very important" to him: creativity, physical activity, autonomy, and variety. Gary also listed the following values as "not important" at all: economic return, prestige, and achievement. On the GATB, Gary had average scores in all of the nine aptitudes except Manual Dexterity, Spatial Aptitude, and Form Perception. On the CEI, Gary scored highest in the Mechanical, Plants, and Protecting areas and scored lowest in the Social Service, Personal Service, and Financial Detail areas.

I reviewed the test scores with Gary at the end of the second session. We talked about his interests first. I questioned him about why he thought that he scored highest in the three areas that he did on the CEI. He said he scored high in Mechanical because he had worked with his hands all of his life, Plants because he liked to garden in his spare time, and Protecting because he was interested in law enforcement—especially weapons and martial arts. On the GATB, he was surprised that he scored so high in Spatial Aptitude and Form Perception. With the values card sort, he said that autonomy and variety were very important to him and that he did not value money or prestige. He also noted, "If I value autonomy and variety and not money, why was I working at that job? I did not have variety or autonomy, and I only worked there because the money was so good!" For the next session, I asked Gary to draw a career rainbow as a homework assignment. He agreed, and I could see that he was starting to have some insights into his career development.

Goal 2: Help the Client Learn More About His Life-Space Issues.

Objectives
1. Examine the client's life structure.
2. Examine the client's role interactions.

Interventions
1. Ask client to complete his career rainbow.

We started the third session by reviewing Gary's career rainbow. The results of the rainbow showed that he was currently involved in a variety of roles including husband, father, leisurite, son, brother, and now homemaker. He was not involved in the worker role or the student role. We talked about how he felt about not working. He said that he was still a little angry at the company and felt like he had been betrayed by them. I spent a considerable amount of time allowing Gary to vent some of his pent-up feelings about his current situation. He expressed some feelings of guilt about not being the "breadwinner" for his family, and he said he felt like he had let his wife down. Because these feelings are the result of irrational thinking, I chose to explore these feelings later in the session.

The career rainbow helps the client explore the variety of roles he is currently playing and examine how these roles are affecting his life satisfaction. I asked Gary to evaluate the number and types of roles he was playing and to evaluate the energy that he was putting into each role. If necessary, I would help him redesign his life so that he would have more life satisfaction. At this point, the only additional role Gary needed to consider was the student role. We talked about his interest in going back to school for more education. Gary stated that he would not mind doing so in the future but that, at the present time, he wanted to try to find a job.

At this point, I returned to the subject of some of the irrational things that Gary was thinking about as we talked.

Goal 3: Correct Irrational and Dysfunctional Beliefs.

Objectives
1. Identify patterns of irrational thinking.

Interventions
1. Monitor the client's self-talk.
2. Assign a "thoughts" journal.
3. Ask for evidence to verify beliefs.

As I talked with Gary, I remained alert for patterns of irrational thinking about himself or the world-of-work. He had already identified some of his irrational thoughts in talking about his guilt over not being the breadwinner and about letting his wife down. I helped the client listen to any negative talk that might be going on in his head. Gary kept a daily journal in which he recorded his self-talk and replaced negative statements with more positive ones. Some of his other irrational thoughts were that "Nobody will hire a man my age" and "I'm too old to learn anything new." I used the results of the battery of tests he completed to help Gary identify and dispute unrealistic beliefs he had about himself. For example, the results of the GATB indicated that he had the ability to go back to school if he wanted to do so and that he had the aptitude to get a number of different jobs. Another way that I helped Gary examine his irrational thinking was by simply asking for examples or evidence to either support or disprove his irrational beliefs.

Goal 4: Gather Realistic Occupational Information.

Objectives
1. Gather information about self and the world-of-work.

Interventions
1. Encourage the client to complete the SIGI+.
2. Help the client explore a variety of sources of occupational information.

At the end of the third session, I introduced Gary to my career information library. I suggested that he spend some time there during the week and complete the SIGI Plus computerized career guidance system. He could also utilize the career information resources such as O*NET, the *Dictionary of Occupational Titles,* and the *Guide for Occupational Exploration.*

I used the occupational information he gathered to identify any misinformation he had about job specifications such as a job's salary, working conditions, employment outlook, and educational or training requirements. I tried to reframe how Gary saw himself and his situation.

Because Gary knew very little about the world-of-work, I started by helping him systematically explore occupational information in which he had aptitudes and interests using a variety of media.

I also suggested that he shadow workers in some of the fields in which he was interested or at least conduct interviews with some of these workers. All this work was to be completed outside the career counseling sessions on the client's own time.

Gary and I started the fourth session by reviewing what he had discovered in his search through occupational information related to his interests and aptitudes. He said he had come across a variety of occupations that really interested him. The list included occupations such as appraiser, cabinetmaker, locksmith, drafter, electrician, and police officer. This seemed to be a very realistic list. We talked about what he liked about each of these occupations. The occupations were similar except one—police officer.

At this point, I thought Gary needed some additional information: specifically, he needed to know how congruent his personality was with each of the occupations in which he was interested. So, I administered the Self-Directed Search (SDS).

Goal 5: Help the Client Understand Aspects of His Personality.

Objectives
1. Identify the congruence, differentiation, and consistency of the client's personality type.

Interventions
1. Administer the Self-Directed Search.

Gary took ten minutes during the session to take the SDS. His three-letter code was Realistic-Investigative-Enterprising (RIE). Using the Career Options Finder for the SDS, I asked Gary to look at the list of occupations listed under RIE first, then possibly REI and IRE, for occupations of interest. He said that there was not much else of interest. I then explored the degree of fit between Gary's "type" and the work environment of all his occupations of interest. Many of the occupations were realistic occupations; however, one occupation—drafting—is listed as an RIE fit. The one occupation in which Gary was interested that was not a good personality fit for him was police officer. Police officer was listed under the occupations for Social individuals. Gary said that he was not very social and crossed that occupation off his list. I also explored the degree of differentiation that his scores showed and talked to Gary about the degree of clarity and stability of his vocational identity. I asked him to bring his list of occupations with him to the next session.

At the start of the fifth session, I wanted to concentrate on decision making. I explored his past decisions in an attempt to identify his decision-making style. It appeared that Gary's decision-making style was somewhat rational, not impulsive. Gary had not made many career-related decisions, however, since he had worked at the same job for twenty-eight years.

Goal 6: Explore the Way the Client Makes Decisions.

Objectives
1. Explore the client's values as they relate to decision making.
2. Help the client identify possible occupational alternatives.

Interventions
1. Teach the client a rational decision-making process.
2. Help the client brainstorm occupational alternatives.
3. Discuss where the client is in the career decision-making process.

I helped Gary to view career decision making as a rational process. I modeled for him a process for making major career and life decisions. I also helped Gary identify as many other alternatives as possible and then eliminate alternatives that were unrealistic or inappropriate. Gary eliminated the appraiser and electrician occupations because they were not appropriate in his eyes. Cabinetmaker was something Gary had interest in, but only as a hobby.

Goal 7: Help the Client Examine His Life Satisfaction.

Objectives
1. Explore the interaction of the domains of the client and the work environment.

Interventions
1. Explore the rewards and opportunities available to the client at work.
2. Discuss the job demands and skills requirements of various occupations.

Gary had now narrowed his list of occupations to locksmith and drafter. He decided to continue to look for a job as a metal press operator, but he thought that a change of occupation might be in order. I then helped him evaluate the fit between his skills and needs and those of each of the occupations of interest. To do so, I administered the Minnesota Importance Questionnaire to measure his work needs and looked at the scores from the GATB that he had taken in a previous testing session. I compared these test results to similar measures of abilities and values needed for occupations by using the Occupational Ability Patterns (OAP) identified on the GATB to assess how well each occupation would meet Gary's needs. Gary identified drafting as an occupation that he wanted to enter. I gave Gary a homework assignment of reading more about the various types of drafting that are available and the requirements to enter this field.

In the last session, I concentrated on how Gary might implement his choice for an occupational change—drafting. He seemed to have a real interest in computer-assisted drafting. He had enrolled during the previous week in a computer-aided drafting program sponsored by the local Department of Labor. He was able to withdraw part of his retirement from the electronics plant to live on while he attended school.

Goal 8: Increase Knowledge of the Effects of Leisure upon Career.

Objectives
1. Explore the client's past, present, and future leisure activities and interests.

Interventions
1. Administer the Career Exploration Inventory and the Leisure/Work Search Inventory.
2. Assist the client in identifying satisfying leisure activities.

I administered the Leisure/Work Search Inventory and started to explore the leisure interests of Gary over his life span. I then finished our counseling sessions by talking to Gary about the importance of having satisfying leisure activities. In his leisure time, Gary enjoyed gardening, martial arts, and woodworking. We talked about the possibility of exploring any leisure interests that might be turned into an occupation, small business, or home-based business. Gary said that woodworking was something he really enjoyed and that he might turn it into a business by selling his finished products.

As the case of Gary illustrates, the treatment planning process is an excellent way for career counselors to assist their clients with career-related problems. Setting appropriate, behaviorally measureable goals is the crucial part of developing a treatment plan. These goals help guide the career counseling process and keep the career counselor and the client focused.

 # REFERENCES

Adler, A. (1956). *The individual psychology of Alfred Adler.* New York: Basic Books.

Adler, A. (1964). *Social interest: A challenge to mankind.* New York: Capricorn Books.

American Psychiatric Association. 1994. *Diagnostic and statistical manual of mental disorders* (4th ed.). Washington, DC: Author.

Bandura, A. (1969). *Principles of behavior modification.* New York: Holt, Rinehart & Winston.

Bandura, A. (1977). *Social learning theory.* Englewood Cliffs, NJ: Prentice-Hall.

Bandura, A. (1986). *Social foundations of thought and action: A social-cognitive theory.* Englewood Cliffs, NJ: Prentice-Hall.

Betz, N. E., & Hackett, G. (1981). The relationship of career-related self-efficacy expectations to perceived career options in college women and men. *Journal of Counseling Psychology, 28*(5), 339–410.

Blau, P. M., & Duncan, O. D. (1967). *The American occupational structure.* New York: Wiley.

Blocher, D. H., & Biggs, D. A. (1983). *Counseling psychology in community settings.* New York: Springer.

Bloland, P. A., & Edwards, P. (1981). Work and leisure: A counseling synthesis. *Vocational Guidance Quarterly, 30*(2), 101–108.

Bolles, R. N. (1988). *The three boxes of life.* Berkeley, CA: Ten Speed Press.

Bordin, E. S. (1968). *Psychological counseling.* New York: Appleton-Century-Crofts.

Bordin, E. S. (1990). Psychodynamic model of career choice and satisfaction. In D. Brown, L. Brooks, & Associates (Eds.), *Career choice and development: Applying contemporary theories to practice* (2d ed., pp. 102–144). San Francisco: Jossey-Bass.

Borgen, F. H., Weiss, D. J., Tinsley, H. E., Dawis, R. V., & Lofquist, L. H. (1968). *Minnesota Job Description Questionnaire.* Minneapolis, MN: University of Minnesota, Work Adjustment Project.

Borow, H. (1982). Career development theory and instrumental outcomes of career guidance. In J. D. Krumboltz & D. A. Hamel (Eds.), *Assessing career development.* Palo Alto, CA: Mayfield.

Bowen, M. (1980). *Key to the genogram.* Washington, DC: Georgetown University Hospital.

Brammer, L. M. (1979). *The helping relationship: Process and skills.* Englewood Cliffs, NJ: Prentice-Hall.

Brenner, M. H. (1973). *Mental illness and the economy.* Cambridge, MA: Harvard University Press.

Brenner, S. O., & Bartell, R. (1983). The psychological impact of unemployment: A structural analysis of cross-sectional data. *Journal of Occupational Psychology, 56,* 129–136.

Bridges, W. (1994, September). The end of the job. *Fortune,* 62–67.

Brown, D. (1985). Career counseling: Before, after, or instead of personal counseling? *The Vocational Guidance Quarterly, 33*(3), 197–201.

Brown, D., & Brooks, L. (1991). *Career counseling techniques.* Needham Heights, MA: Allyn & Bacon.

Brown, D., & Minor, C. W. (1992). *Working in America: A status report on planning and problems.* Washington, DC: National Career Development Association and National Occupational Information Coordinating Committee.

Charland, W. (1993). *Career shifting: Starting over in a changing economy.* Holbrook, MA: Adams.

Cheatham, H. E. (1990). Africentricity and career development of African Americans. *The Career Development Quarterly, 38*(4), 334–346.

Clarridge, B. R., Sheehy, L. L., & Hauser, T. S. (1977). Tracing members of a panel: A seventeen-year follow-up. In K. F. Schussler (Ed.), *Sociological methodology.* San Francisco: Jossey-Bass.

Cochran, L. (1997). *Career counseling: A narrative approach.* Thousand Oaks, CA: Sage.

Crites, J.O. (1973). *Career Maturity Inventory.* Monterey, CA: California Test Bureau/McGraw-Hill.

Crites, J. O. (1981). *Career counseling: Models, methods, and materials.* New York: McGraw-Hill.

Csikszentmihalyi, M. (1990). *Flow: The psychology of optimal experience.* New York: Harper & Row.

Dawis, R. V. (1992). Individual differences tradition in counseling psychology. *Journal of Counseling Psychology, 39,* 7–19.

Dawis, R. V., England, G. W., & Lofquist, L. H. (1964). A theory of work adjustment. Minneapolis, MN: University of Minnesota Industrial Relations Center.

Dawis, R. V., & Lofquist, L. (1984). *A psychological theory of work adjustment: An individual differences model and its application.* Minneapolis, MN: University of Minnesota.

Day, L. (1996). *Practical intuition.* New York: Broadway Books.

Dillard, J. M. (1985). *Lifelong career planning.* Columbus, OH: Merrill.

Emery, M. (1994). *Intuition workbook.* Englewood Cliffs, NJ: Prentice-Hall.

Farr, J. M. (1996). *Manual for The Guide for Occupational Exploration Inventory.* Indianapolis, IN: JIST.

Feather, N. T., & Davenport, P. R. (1981). Unemployment and depressive affect: A motivational and attributional analysis. *Journal of Personality and Social Psychology, 41,* 422–436.

Fredrickson, R. H. (1982). *Career information.* Englewood Cliffs, NJ: Prentice-Hall.

Gainor, K. A., & Forrest, L. (1991). African American women's self-concept: Implications for career decisions and career counseling. *The Career Development Quarterly, 39*(3), 261–272.

Gati, I. (1986). Making career decisions—A sequential elimination approach. *Journal of Counseling Psychology, 33,* 408–417.

Gati, I., Fassa, N., & Houminer, D. (1995). Applying decision theory to career counseling practice: The sequential elimination approach. *Career Development Quarterly, 43,* 211–220.

Gawain, S. (1978). *Creative visualization.* New York: Bantam.

Gelatt, H. B. (1962). Decision making: A conceptual frame of reference for counseling. *Journal of Counseling Psychology, 32*(9), 252–256.

Gelatt, H. B. (1989). Positive uncertainty: A new decision-making framework for counseling. *Journal of Counseling Psychology, 9,* 240–245.

Ginter, G. G. (1995). *Systematic treatment planning with an overview of DSM-IV.* Workshop presented at the annual meeting of the American Counseling Association.

Ginzberg, E. (1972). Toward a theory of occupational choice: A restatement. *Vocational Guidance Quarterly, 20,* 169–176.

Ginzberg, E. (1984). Career development. In D. Brown & L. Brooks (Eds.), *Career choice and development* (pp. 169–191). San Francisco: Jossey-Bass.

Ginzberg, E., Ginsburg, S. A., Axelrad, S., & Herma, J. L. (1951). *Occupational choice: An approach to a general theory.* New York: Columbia University Press.

Gysbers, N. C., & Associates. (1984). *Designing careers counseling to enhance education, work, and leisure.* San Francisco: Jossey-Bass.

Gysbers, N. C., Heppner, M. J., & Johnston, J. A. (1998). *Career counseling: Process, issues, and techniques.* Needham Heights, MA: Allyn & Bacon.

Gysbers, N. C., & Moore, E. J. (1987). *Career counseling: Skills and techniques for practitioners.* Englewood Cliffs, NJ: Prentice-Hall.

Hackett, R. D. (1985). The role of mathematics self-efficacy in choice of math-related majors of college men and women: A path analysis. *Journal of Counseling Psychology, 32,* 47–56.

Hackett, R. D., & Betz, N. E. (1981). A self-efficacy approach to the career development of women. *Journal of Vocational Behavior, 18,* 326–329.

Hansen L. S. (1997). *Integrative life planning.* San Francisco: Jossey-Bass.

Hawks, B. K., & Muha, D. (1991). Facilitating the career development of minorities: Doing it differently this time. *The Career Development Quarterly, 39*(3), 251–260.

Herr, E. L., & Cramer, S. H. (1984). *Career guidance and counseling through the life span* (2d ed.). Boston: Little, Brown.

Hershenson, D. B. (1974). Vocational guidance and the handicapped. In E. L. Herr (Ed.), *Vocational guidance and human development* (pp. 478–501). Boston: Houghton Mifflin.

Hershenson, D. B. (1981). Work adjustment, disability, and the three r's of vocational rehabilitation: A conceptual model. *Rehabilitation Counseling Bulletin, 25,* 91–97.

Hershenson, D. B. (1996). Work adjustment: A neglected area in career counseling. *Journal of Counseling and Development, 74,* 442–446.

Hines, A. (1994). Jobs and infotech: Work in the information society, *Futurist, 28,* 9–13.

Holland, J. L. (1973). *Making vocational choices: A theory of careers.* Englewood Cliffs, NJ: Prentice-Hall.

Holland, J. L. (1977). *Manual for the Vocational Preference Inventory.* Palo Alto, CA: Consulting Psychologists Press.

Holland, J. L. (1979). *Self-directed search.* Palo Alto, CA: Consulting Psychologists Press.

Holland, J. L. (1980). *My vocational situation.* Palo Alto, CA: Consulting Psychologists Press.

Holland, J. L. (1992). *Making vocational choices.* Odessa, FL: Psychological Assessment Resources.

Hoppock, R. (1976). *Occupational information*. New York: McGraw-Hill.

Hotchkiss, L., & Borow, H. (1990). Sociological perspectives on work and career. In D. Brown & L. Brooks (Eds.), *Career choice and development* (2d ed., pp. 262–307). San Francisco: Jossey-Bass.

Imbimbo, P. V. (1994). Integrating personal and career counseling: A challenge for counselors. *Journal of Employment Counseling, 31,* 50–59.

Isaacson, L. E., & Brown, D. (1993). *Career information, career counseling, and career development* (6th Ed.). Boston: Allyn & Bacon.

Isaacson, L. E., & Brown, D. (1997). *Career information, career counseling, and career development* (7th Ed.). Boston: Allyn & Bacon.

Ivey, A. (1994). *Intentional interviewing and counseling*. Pacific Grove, CA: Brooks/Cole.

Jepsen, D. A. (1984). Relationship between career development theory and practice. In N. C. Gysbers (Ed.), *Designing careers: Counseling to enhance education, work, and leisure* (pp. 135–159). San Francisco: Jossey-Bass.

Jones, W. H. (1979). Grief and involuntary career change: Its implications for counseling. *Vocational Guidance Quarterly, 27,* 196–201.

Jongsma, A. E., & Peterson, L. M. (1995). *The complete psychotherapy treatment planner*. New York: Wiley.

Jung, C. (1923). *Psychological types*. New York: Harcourt Brace.

Katz, M. R. (1966). A model of guidance for career decision making. *Vocational Guidance Quarterly, 15,* 2–10.

Kleibert, D., Larson, L., & Csikszentmihalyi, M. (1986). The experience of leisure in adolescence. *Journal of Leisure Research, 18,* 169–176.

Krumboltz, J. D. (1979). A social learning theory of career decision making. In A. M. Mitchell, G. B. Jones, & J. D. Krumboltz (Eds.), *Social learning and career decision making*. Cranston, RI: Carroll Press.

Krumboltz, J. D. (1983). *Private rules in career decision making*. Columbus, OH: National Center for Research in Vocational Education.

Krumboltz, J. D. (1991). *Career beliefs inventory*. Palo Alto, CA: Consulting Psychologists Press.

Krumboltz, J. D. (1994). Improving career development theory from a social learning theory perspective. In M. L. Savickas & R. W. Lent (Eds.), *Convergence in career development theory* (pp. 9–32). Palo Alto, CA: Consulting Psychologists Press.

Law, J., Moracco, J., & Wilmarth, R. R. (1981). A problem-oriented record system for counselors. *American Mental Health Counselor's Association Journal, 3*(1), 7–16.

Lent, R. W., Brown, S. D., & Hackett, G. (1994). Toward a unifying social cognitive theory of career and academic interest, choice, and performance. *Journal of Vocational Behavior, 45,* 79–122.

Leong, F. T. L. (1991). Career development attributes and occupational values of Asian American and white college students. *The Career Development Quarterly, 39*(3), 221–230.

Liptak, J. J. (1990). Pre-retirement counseling: Integrating the leisure planning component. *The Career Development Quarterly, 38*(4), 360–367.

Liptak, J. J. (1991a). Leisure and work. In L. K. Jones (Ed.), *The encyclopedia of career decision and work issues*. Phoenix, AZ: Oryx Press.

Liptak, J. J. (1991b). Leisure counseling: An antidote to the living death. *Journal of Employment Counseling, 28*(3), 115–120.

Liptak, J. J. (1991c). The fourth alternative: Leisure search and planning. *Journal of Employment Counseling, 28*(2), 57–62.

Liptak, J. J. (1992a). The CEI: Expanding options for the unemployed. *Journal of Employment Counseling, 29*(2), 60–68.

Liptak, J. J. (1992b). *Manual for the Career Exploration Inventory.* Indianapolis, IN: JIST.

Liptak, J. J. (1994a). *Manual for the Job Search Attitudes Inventory.* Indianapolis, IN: JIST.

Liptak, J. J. (1994b). *Manual for the Leisure Search Inventory.* Indianapolis, IN: JIST.

Liptak, J. J. (1996). *Manual for the Barriers to Employment Success Inventory.* Indianapolis, IN: JIST.

Liptak, J. J. (1998). *CEI workshop: Fusing work and leisure.* Dover, DE: Center for Career Assessment.

Maslow, A. H. (1968). *Toward a psychology of being.* New York: Van Nostrand.

Maslow, A. H. (1971). *The farther reaches of human nature.* New York: Penguin.

Maxmen, J. S., & Ward, N. G. (1995). *Essential psychopathology and its treatment.* New York: Norton.

McDaniels, C. (1984). The role of leisure in career development. *Journal of Career Development, 11*(2), 64–70.

McDaniels, C. (1989). *The changing workplace: Career counseling strategies for the 1990s and beyond.* San Francisco: Jossey-Bass.

McDaniels, C., & Gysbers, N. C. (1992). *Counseling for career development.* San Francisco: Jossey-Bass.

Miller, V. M. (1999). The opportunity structure: Implications for career counseling. *Journal of Employment Counseling, 36*(1), 2–12.

Mirvis, P. H., & Hall, D. T. (1994). Psychological success and the boundaryless career. *Journal of Organizational Behavior, 15,* 365–380.

National Vocational Guidance Association. (1982). *The position paper on career development.* Falls Church, VA: Author.

Novak, J. (1989). *How to meditate.* Nevada City, CA: Crystal Clarity.

O'Brien, G. E., & Kabanoff, B. (1979). Comparison of unemployed and employed workers on work values, locus of control and health variables. *Australian Psychologist, 14,* 143–154.

Okiishi, R. W. (1987). The genogram as a tool in career counseling. *Journal of Counseling and Development, 66*(3), 139–143.

Osipow, S. (1983). *Theories of career development.* Englewood Cliffs, NJ: Prentice-Hall.

Parker, M. (1991). Career and employment counseling with Soviet Jewish immigrants: Issues and recommendations. *Journal of Employment Counseling, 28*(4), 157–166.

Parsons, F. (1909). *Choosing a vocation.* Boston: Houghton Mifflin.

Pearson, Q. M. (1998). Job satisfaction, leisure satisfaction, and psychological health. *Career Development Quarterly, 46*(4), 416–426.

Peterson, G. W., Sampson, J. P., & Reardon, R. C. (1991). *Career development and services: A cognitive approach.* Pacific Grove, CA: Brooks/Cole.

Platt, S. (1984). Unemployment and suicidal behavior: A review of the literature. *Social Science Medicine, 19,* 93–115.

Read, N. O., Elliot, M. R., Escobar, M. D., & Slaney, R. B. (1988). The effects of marital status and motherhood on the career concerns of reentry women. *The Career Development Quarterly, 37*(1), 46–55.

Rifkin, J. (1995). *The end of work: Technology, jobs, and your future.* New York: Putnam.

Roe, A. (1956). *The psychology of occupations.* New York: Wiley.

Roe, A. (1972). Perspectives on vocational development. In J. M. Whiteley & A. Resnikoff (Eds.), *Perspectives on vocational development.* Washington, DC: American Personnel and Guidance Association.

Roe, A., & Siegelman, M. (1964). *The origins of interests.* Washington, DC: American Personnel and Guidance Association.

Rogers, C. S., & Sawyers, J. K. (1988). *Play in the lives of children.* Washington, DC: National Association for the Education of Young Children.

Rounds, J. B., Henley, G. A., Dawis, R. V., Lofquist, L. H., & Weiss, D. J. (1981). *Manual for the Minnesota Importance Questionnaire.* Minneapolis, MN: University of Minnesota, Work Adjustment Project.

Sears, S. (1982). A definition of career guidance terms: A National Vocational Guidance Association perspective. *Vocational Guidance Quarterly, 31*(2), 137–143.

Seligman, L. (1993). Teaching treatment planning. *Counselor Education and Supervision, 33*(4), 297–297.

Seligman, L. (1994). *Developmental career counseling and assessment.* Thousand Oaks, CA: Sage.

Seligman, L. (1996). *Diagnosis and treatment planning in counseling.* New York: Plenum.

Sewell, W. H., Haller, A. O., & Portes, A. (1969). The educational and occupational aspiration. *American Sociological Review, 22,* 67–73.

Sharf, R. S. (1997). *Applying career development theory to counseling.* Pacific Grove, CA: Brooks/Cole.

Sinfield, A. (1981). *What unemployment means.* Oxford, England: Martin Robertson.

Spokane, A. R. (1991). *Career interventions.* Englewood Cliffs, NJ: Prentice-Hall.

Staines, G. L. (1980). Spillover versus compensation: A review of the literature on the relationship between work and nonwork. *Human Relations, 33*(2), 111–129.

Stark, M. (1998). Misery or mastery: Treatment planning in Christian counseling. *Christian Counseling Today, 5*(4), 9–12.

Super, D. E. (1940). *Avocational interest patterns.* New York: Columbia Teachers College Press.

Super, D. E. (1951). Vocational adjustment: Implementing a self-concept. *Occupations,* 10, 88–92.

Super, D. E. (1953). A theory of vocational development. *American Psychologist, 8,* 185–190.

Super, D. E. (1976). *Career education and the meanings of work.* Washington, DC: U.S. Government Printing Office.

Super, D. E. (1980). A life-span, life-space approach to career development. *Journal of Vocational Behavior, 16,* 282–298.

Super, D. E. (1981). A developmental theory: Implementing a self-concept. In D. H. Montross & C. J. Shinkman (Eds.), *Career development in the 1980s: Theory and practice.* Springfield, IL: Thomas.

Super, D. E. (1985). Coming of age in Middletown. *American Psychologist, 40*(4), 405–414.

Super, D. E. (1986). Life career roles: Self-realization in work and leisure. In D. T. Hall & Associates (Eds.), *Career development in organizations*. San Francisco: Jossey-Bass.

Super, D. E. (1990). A life-span, life-space approach to career development. In D. Brooks & L. Brown (Eds.), *Career choice and development: Applying contemporary theories to practice*. San Francisco: Jossey-Bass.

Super, D. E., & Bachrach, P. (1957). *Scientific careers and vocational development theory*. New York: Teachers College Press.

Super, D. E., & Harris-Bowlsbey, J. A. (1979). *Guided career exploration*. New York: Psychological Corporation.

Super, D. E., & Nevill, D. D. (1985). *The Salience Inventory*. Palo Alto, CA: Consulting Psychologists Press.

Super, D. E., Thompson, A. S., & Lindeman, R. E. (1988). *Adult Career Concerns Inventory*. Palo Alto, CA: Consulting Psychologists Press.

Super, D. E., Thompson, A. S., Lindeman, R. E., Jordaan, J. P., & Meyers, R. A. (1981). *Career Development Inventory*. Palo Alto, CA: Consulting Psychologists Press.

Tiedeman, A. M. (1988). *Lifecareer: The quantum leap into a process theory of career*. Vista, CA: Lifecareer Foundation.

Tiedeman, D. V., & Miller-Tiedeman, A. (1984). Career decision making: An individual's perspective. In D. Brown & L. Brooks (Eds.), *Career choice and development*. San Francisco: Jossey-Bass.

Tiedeman, D. V., & O'Hara, R. (1963). *Career development: Choice and adjustment*. New York: Entrance Examination Board.

U.S. Department of Labor. (1982). *Manual for the USES General Aptitude Battery*. Washington, DC: U.S. Government Printing Office.

U.S. Department of Labor. (1993, Fall). The American work force, 1992–2005. *Occupational Outlook Quarterly*. Washington, DC: U.S. Government Printing Office.

Vaughan, F. (1979). *Awakening intuition*. Garden City, NY: Anchor.

Warr, P. B., Jackson, P. R., & Banks, M. H. (1982). Duration of unemployment and psychological well-being in young men and women. *Current Psychological Research, 2,* 207–214.

Watkins, C. E., Jr., & Savickas, M. L. (1990). Psychodynamic career counseling. In W. B. Walsh & S. H. Osipow (Eds.), *Career counseling: Contemporary topics in vocational psychology* (pp. 79–116). Hillsdale, NJ: Erlbaum.

Weeks, E. C., & Drencacz, S. (1983). Rocking in a small boat: The consequences of economic change in rural communities. *International Journal of Mental Health, 23,* 62–75.

Winegardner, D., Simonetti, J. L., & Nykodym, N. (1984). Unemployment: The living death? *Journal of Employment Counseling, 21,* 149–155.

Yost, E. B., & Corbishley, M. A. (1987). *Career counseling: A psychological approach*. San Francisco: Jossey-Bass.

Zunker, V. G. (1994). *Career counseling: Applied concepts of life planning*. Pacific Grove, CA: Brooks/Cole.